MW00713316

Perfect
Balance
Golf

Perfect Balance Golf

Your Key to Consistency and Shot Making in Golf

Bob Cisco

Editor: Alan Gilbertson
Illustrations: Ann Fewell
Book and Cover Design: Alan Gilbertson
G&G Creative Productions, Tujunga, CA

ISBN 978-0-9635097 27

Printed in United States of America
Pre-publication edition

Book design by Alan Gilbertson, G&G Creative, Los Angeles

Dedication

This book is dedicated to all those who love and have a passion for the game and to these teachers and instructors for their legacy and contributions to the game of golf:

Tommy Armour	*George Knudsen*
Jim Ballard	*David Leadbetter*
Peggy Kirk Bell	*Davis Love, Jr.*
Patty Berg	*Stuart Maiden*
Percy Boomer	*Jim McLain*
Jackie Burke Jr.	*Eddie Merrins*
Henry Cotton	*Byron Nelson*
Manuel de la Torre	*Johnny Revolta*
Gardner Dickinson	*Harvey Penick*
Jim Flick	*Paul Runyan*
Ellen Griffin	*Sir Walter Simpson*
Jack Grout	*Sam Snead*
Jim Hardy	*Bob Toski*
Claude Harmon	*Harry Vardon*
Butch Harmon	*Ken Venturi*
John Jacobs	*Kathy Whitworth*
Ernest Jones	*Earl Woods*

Bob Cisco, 2007

Contents

Introduction

In 2004, I made a discovery that would prove to be bigger than any I had previously made about the true nature of the golf swing. Not only did it provide a personal revelation to me as a golfer, it was a discovery that would impact the entire direction of instruction of the golf swing. It would also allow for the formulation of a workable system of instruction for golfers which would change the face of golf instruction as we know it today.

I would like to tell you how this came about and the story behind it, but there is actually more than one story: two stories that came together somewhere towards the end of this road. Although the road had various directions and sometimes veered off on its own, in the end things looked familiar in their basic design, but with some new pieces present, reassembled, strengthened in application and given a new, more meaningful purpose and look.

The first story has to do with the question (and if you are like most golfers, you have asked this many times): "Why are advanced players and top pros able to play far better than other golfers, even those who have equal athletic ability?"

How is it that the pros play at the level that they play to, while the rest of golfers, in their frustration, don't break the 100 score?

For years as a player and instructor, I knew there had to be a technique, a blend of key moves that a golfer had to produce in each shot to consistently hit good shots to the target. Things like rhythm, timing and balance are vital in the golf swing — swing plane and path. But of these basics, was there one that was more important than the others; one key to your swing and success?

Players, golfers and (in older days when courses had them) caddies would often congregate and talk of key swing moves that the legendary players made, great moments when the game's greats hit towering drives and fairway woods over trees and lakes and holed out shots to win matches and golf tournaments, legends like Jones, Snead, Hogan, Nelson, Palmer, Nicklaus and Tiger Woods.

These stories were sometimes concocted from myth in clubhouse pubs or nearby local taverns, often over too much beer, but still the same stories were told and continued to create a belief that they were true and could be learned from. Interest in them continued, to be renewed or passed down to new golfers in tale and fable.

These stories, and the old golf books I read as a golfer and instructor looking for the "truth of the golf swing", always held my curiosity: what if there were a fundamental swing move that could be identified and tapped, not just in some late night pub down the street from the golf course, or in the inner circle of golf academia, but made available for all golfers to have and use in their game?

Commentators talked about great balance and timing of golfing greats. Key instructors talked about the importance of swinging the club head (Ernest Jones), a drop down or "magic move" in the forward swing back to the ball (Harvey Pennick), but no one had really studied the keys to balance or how balance might be the true basis and real natural truth to this drop-down move in the accelerated attack at the ball. Could this be a realistic premise to explore?

So my second question had to do with a "special move" the advanced player and pro made in his down swing that created the proper release at impact, that unleashed an effortless power allowing the shaft to work its magic in the hitting area at the ball.

One of the common threads to the endless stories and tales of super golf shots was this 'drop-down' move, of harnessing effortless power in the down swing.

Was there a special downward pull of the club head at the ball? And if there was such a "magic move", did only the advanced player know how to do it? Did he then keep it to himself as his own secret, what with golf being a highly competitive game?

To my disappointment, no one in instructional circles had really tapped or worked this out. How each player made this move and initiated it seemed to be different and highly individual. Instructors and students all seemed to have their own take on this.

This "special move" would incorporate the key actions of the golf swing. It would produce the "all-in-one" motion.

We all have heard about the importance of a one piece takeaway in the backswing. But what about a one piece all-encompassing motion? It would have to be powerful yet simple and have all the ingredients in the lineup like tempo, rhythm and timing working together, be easy to grasp, able be learned and to be taught.

I got even more excited about the possibility that 'balance' could be the real truth or "real deal" in the golf swing, one that has been truly overlooked.

Perhaps there was something special secret about how balance and rotation were performed in the golf swing that made the difference between an average golfer and an advanced player or pro.

There had to be something seriously wrong or overlooked with the existing scene: despite many new golfers coming into the game, about the same number were leaving the game out of sheer frustration.

So I decided, as a former PGA tour instructor who has worked with pros on all of the major tours, to tackle this area and to fully investigate not only why the national average was so high and why instructors were failing in their mission as teachers, but to take on this challenge to look for and find the "real deal" — that special all encompassing move or motion. In doing so I became fascinated with the challenge of finding the real key move and action in the golf swing.

This book tells you what I have found in my research over a ten year period, and especially since those first days a few years ago. I think you will be pleasantly surprised, as I was, to find the truth about the golf swing.

This is a road that leads back to a true fundamental that has been Missing In Action, a timeless and classic approach to the golf swing, that ties together the key basics that power the swing. It provides the key that opens the door to your full understanding of the swing.

Join me now and travel back in time as I reveal the lost secret of the swing and a new "golf discovery" that will take your game to a new level, a true secret from golf's instructional masters, left on tattered notes and pages in old golf manuscripts, and in passed down descriptions of golf wisdom.

To all my fellow golfers: welcome back, and may your game never be the same.

The new motto in the game of golf improvement is Rotational Balance. It is based on the recent discovery of the balance principle of golf! We are rethinking the golf swing, and we celebrate a return to golf's golden age of instruction.

The primary focus regarding the improvement of the golf swing is balance.

Our motto and mission: IMPROVING YOUR BALANCE IMPROVES YOUR SWING AND THUS YOUR GAME!

The impact of this discovery and the emergence of a new teaching model continue to amaze me in its effectiveness. The simplicity of this teaching model is making it a leader in the instructional world, and with the golfers in the pilot programs we are conducting in our golf schools.

It is not a new thought that golfers utilize balance in the golf swing. It *is* a new thought that he operates or focuses on *balance* as the key basic or fundamental to swing motion. That's what we are interested in here.

So we needed a new word or coined phrase, to capture or explain the essence of this basic and we call it, in our Perfect Balance System, "rotational balance."

For the first time in many years we now have a workable system that can work for students and more advanced golfers to reach a higher level of skill and more enjoyment of their games.

This discovery is supported in application by a new set of principles taken from my latest research on the key role of rotational balance in golf.

Golf is a game of maintaining balance in the hitting of the golf shot. Until now, this fact hasn't been extensively examined and taught in a method that focuses on its importance to the golf swing. If you want golf shots that are consistently good, you need to change your mindset about what is important in shot-making. You need to know that better balance is your key in acquiring consistency. Improved balance means better scores.

Here, then, are the principles and practice of *Perfect Balance: Your Key to Consistency and Shot-Making in Golf.*

The purpose of this work is to assist golfers and instructors to achieve more consistent results in learning and teaching golf, with the major goal of lowering the existing national average scores for all golfers, male and female.

An additional purpose to this book is the rekindling of golf's instructional heritage — its key basics — and a return to the golden age of golf. What did these instructors know that they failed to pass on? And how were they able to create more champions than at any other period in golf history, despite a considerable difference in golf equipment?

Is there a way to reach more of our potential, play smarter and learn more enjoyable golf, to have a significant advantage, to possess the "dynamic and perfectly balanced" golf swing?

The answer is Yes! There is a better way and you *can learn* the physical "feel" of the game and tap the balance connection to golf.

You can play better, smarter and more enjoyable golf, and not only astonish your golfing friends, but play far beyond your current level. You can achieve goals in your game that you only dreamed were possible. We have many reports of players doing just that, with testimonials and successes flooding in.

The "Perfect Balance" golfer is one who possesses and is skilled in the most advanced technology of balance and sports motion ever assembled, and who knows his fundamentals cold. He can improve not only his consistency and ball striking skills, but can be focused, with a decisive mental game. He can "think smart" and relax under pressure. He plays to his potential and can continue to improve.

There are two major sections to this book. Your journey begins on the next page. Each section is written with comprehensive and proven information to rocket you and your game to the success you know you are truly capable of reaching in golf.

This introduction and Section I address the problem in golf instruction today, the discovery of the missing link in the golf swing, and the return to golf's golden era of key basics. Section I also provides cutting edge information on the need for an effective solution, and why Perfect Balance is the instructional model that works best.

Section II covers additional theory and essential drills to master Perfect Balance and introduces the balance principle to golf, along with key information on the role of dynamic balance and swing motion.

The return to traditional basics and new ground-breaking information on "perfect balance in the golf swing" will bridge the past with the future, unlocking the power of simplicity in golf and the scoring potential of the individual golfer.

You have a choice to continue with a mechanical golf model you have been taught, steeped in technical swing positions and a multitude of mechanics, producing a national average over one hundred for men and women — or create a higher potential of gain, understanding and enjoyment of the game by learning the new Perfect Balance method based on the natural laws of motion.

Part 1

Perfect Balance: Your Key to Consistency and Shot Making in Golf

Chapter 1

The New Balance Principle of the Golf Swing

THE PRIMARY ACTION of the golf swing is: Swing the club in balance! Balance and swing motion act together interdependently.

The name of the game in the golf swing is BALANCE. That is the motto of *Perfect Balance in the Golf Swing* and golf's New Motto!

The greatest golfers were all believers in one thing: Swinging the club head in a balanced way, not letting the mechanics of it get in the way or over-thinking how to make the swing. The best players swung the club head and let the club do what it is designed to do. They created rotation and swing motion, hitting the ball with an effortless sense of power, never forcing, complementing the force of gravity.

The first great masters of the game knew that golf as a game had one primary objective and that was "To hit the ball!"

"There is only one categorical imperative in golf and that is to hit the ball. There are no minor absolutes." *The Art of Golf* by Sir Walter Simpson, 1887.

Each golfer has, to a greater or lesser degree, a unique sense of timing and ability to hit the golf ball. The degree he can do that and be consistent with his approach determines the result of his swing and intention. From pro to beginner the mission is the same: to hit the ball with effortless power and control, to play to one's full potential and master the game of golf.

The purpose and function of the golf swing is to enable the player to swing the club and body in rotational, balanced motion.

The great Sam Snead, one of the best swingers of the golf club of all time, would swing a golf club each day one hundred times to practice timing and swinging the club. Much like a concert pianist working the scales to exercise his mastery of the basics and to keep the muscles in rhythmic tune, many of golf's top players used this system to keep their games sharp and focused on the essentials of balance and timing in the golf swing.

Golf, like most sports, requires that you be balanced and as comfortable as possible at all times for maximum efficiency.

"*Balance in motion* is important in any golf shot. In taking up your stance, your weight should be evenly balanced between both feet, and in each foot evenly balanced between the ball and heel of the foot." (Sam Snead, *Natural Golf*, pp. 33 and 48)

The golf swing is a movement of controlled balance. You will find with all advanced players a keen sense of footwork, sensing the swing from the ground up, flowing out through the larger component parts of the body to the arms and hands.

The greatest golfer of the twentieth century and possibly of all time, Jack Nicklaus, said it best: "The golf swing is swung between the arches" [of the feet] and "All timing, distance, and direction comes out of the lower body with the feet leading the way"

Pro golfer George Knudson, considered by Jack Nicklaus "the man with the million dollar swing," stated that the mission of the golfer was "to develop feel from balance" and in doing so swing the club and body in a balanced manner together. How well said!—A poetry in golf motion.

> **Axiom 2:** *Balance is the cornerstone of the golf swing motion. From start to completion, control of the swing depends upon balance. This holds true for all rotational sports that use a club, bat, stick or racquet.*

"Balance governs the swing motion. The better balanced we are, the better our chances are of producing a fluid swing motion. ... We will create consistency and power only if we maintain balance throughout the entire motion." (George Knudson with Lorne Rubenstein, *The Natural Golf Swing*, Section on "The Importance of Balance," p. 58)

Master Instructor, Ernest Jones: "When you swung the club head, balance was a result. ... To play great golf, all one had to do was swing the club head. ... Generating a swinging motion creates centrifugal force and perfect balance." (Ernest Jones, *Swing the Club Head*, 1937) Right on.

Golfing great, Sam Snead: "Balance is important in any golf shot and so in taking up your stance your weight should be evenly balanced between both feet, and in each foot evenly balanced between the ball and heel of the foot." (Sam Snead, *Natural Golf*, p. 33)

Masters Champion, Fred Couples: "Good balance is absolutely essential in any golf swing." (Fred Couples, *Total Shot Making*, p. 168) Couples is golf's modern exemplar of rhythm and balance in the game.

I'll say it again: the name of the game in the golf swing is BALANCE and that is the motto of *Perfect Balance in the Golf Swing*, and golf's New Motto!

All right. We have it from some of the great teachers and players of the game: how they felt about the swing as a motion, with balance as the key that allows any golfer to hit the ball long and straight. This gives us a look and a clue to the role of balance as the primary 'engine' or 'driving force' in the swinging of the golf club and harnessing effortless power.

The discussion of balance and its chief role in the golf swing is the central theme of this work. Newly discovered information on the fundamentals of pivot and footwork will also be covered in very specific detail.

We hear comments all the time, from the commentator's booth to the golf course, about the effects of balance in the golf swing. "He had good balance and the shot was good, and "You were off balance in your swing and the results were inconsistent and poor."

You kind of know when you hit it right - the shot felt good and the result was favorable. A good shot was the result of being balanced in the swing.

Shortly, you will have an opportunity to rate yourself on your balance and what you can do to improve it (Balance and Motion Questionnaire).

Here are a few of the questions:

- ❧ How do you rate yourself on balance? (Not just golf but in life and sports).

- ❧ Do you tend to lose your balance in your golf swing in a particular direction, like backward, to the side or forward? Or a combination of the above?

- ❧ Do you tend to hit the ball from your back leg on your forward swing to the target?

- ❧ Do you shift your weight too quickly going back in your takeaway?

- ❧ Do you feel or do others comment that you "hit from the top" or come over the top in your golf swing?

- ❧ When taking the club back in your backswing, do you swing quickly to the inside with a relatively big hip turn?

- ❧ Can you make a golf swing and maintain your balance at swing's completion for a second or two?

- ❧ In your downswing, do you have to quickly slide your lower body, especially the hips and legs, towards the ball and target?

- ❧ Upon completing your swing, are you on balance and in a resting position or can't hold a balance finish?

- ❧ How aware are you of using footwork in the hitting of your golf shots?

Along with the above questions there are a number of balance awareness exercises, or drills, in the book. Here is a preview: an actual balance drill you can quickly do right now to determine how well you balance with your golf swing.

Stand up and take your golf stance. Let your hands hang down. Rock your weight slightly forward towards your toes and rock back towards your heels. It's natural for your balance to settle towards the middle part of the feet. Your weight should be centered more towards the middle and ball of the foot region of both feet. You should feel athletic and ready for action.

Now move your weight towards your toes and feel how the weight is shifted too far forward. Now move your weight back towards your heels. Then shift your weight towards the middle.

You will find the ideal position is to set up with your weight centered on the middle and ball region of the foot, spread evenly between the left and right foot. A bit more weight on the forefoot is the correct feeling and position with the foot for the golf swing

The complete Balance and Motion test is on page 54.

Rotational Balance is a powerful new concept in golf

Rotational balance is a new principle that has emerged in my latest golf research over the last five years or so with why golfer's continue to manifest inconsistency with their golf swings and also answers why golfers either make the right move or don't in their swings and become advance golfers or remain stuck at the recreational level.

But before we carry on in that direction, we first need to go back and investigate the existing scene in golf instruction: where it came from and where it is leading.

The teaching of the golf swing has emphasized the wrong things.

Despite all the new technological improvements in golf equipment and ball design and the ability to hit the ball longer and straighter, golfers are not improving their consistency in shot making. Scores have continued at the same level for the last 50 years.

In order to hit for effortless power, the golfer has to be able to accelerate the swinging club head downward in the forward swing. The majority of golfers can not do this effectively as a correct action and come "over the top" in the swing instead and end up losing power, hitting a slice or pull left without getting the right feel to pull the club down from the top using their lower bodies.

The real error in this inability to make the correct move in the downswing begins at an earlier point: the backswing move away from the ball. It has been found that eighty percent of all swing errors occur in the first 2–3 feet of the golf swing! Coming over the top in the downswing move is caused by a faulty sense of balance and timing in the rotation of the body and the club.

The amount of inconsistency in ball striking is proportional to the degree of deviation in rotational balance, which depends upon rotation of the body, rotation of the club head, and the *timing of both these rotations*. This is why timing is so important in the swing motion. (More on this later in the text).

Let me explain further with the use of the following illustrations:

At Swing Position 1 you can see the difference in a good golfer's backswing move (Figure 1) and that of a golfer who has trouble breaking 100 (Figure 2). Notice the difference in the vertical line I've drawn of both golfers' hips. The advanced golfer has moved his swing center over the right inner thigh of the back leg and foot whereas the inexperienced golfers has not. The deviation is already quite noticeable.

Golfers have lacked information about a key basic that has been Missing In Action for some time in golf instruction. They have not learned this because instructors who espoused purely mechanical theories did not know how to teach it.

Hidden amongst the true fundamentals of the golf swing is a piece of information having to do with the role of *balance* that never made it into modern golf instruction. It relates to the physics of motion.

To give an example that is easy to follow, imagine the following scenario. You are watching the Olympics. The event is the hammer-throw, in which the athlete throws or heaves a weighted ball on a chain through the air for distance.

He swings the ball around his body a number of times in an effort to gain momentum and velocity to release the hammer and send it down the line to a target in the field a hundred feet or so away.

How does he do this with an object that weighs several pounds?

The speed of the ball comes from the combined effort of the arm-swinging motion and rotation of the body around an axis point or base. The base, the feet and lower body, must remain steady as it rotates. Both the swinging object and the body must be in complete coordination; when one is too fast it affects the other, making the ball fall short or fly out of the correct line.

There is a basic principle at work here that has to do with the interaction of two factors that dominate the golf swing: *rotation* and *balance*.

Try swinging a ball around your body on the end of a rope. You will immediately find that you have to coordinate the swinging of your arms along

with the rotation of your body as the ball gains momentum in its swing. If you swing your arms and hands too quickly or forcibly, you lose the connection between the base (the body) and the ball, and lose control of the rotation and speed.

This little exercise is actually a good way to get the feel of swinging a golf club correctly.

Golfing great Bobby Jones discovered a similar principle in the law of gravity as it applies to the swing. Jones observed that the speed of the club going up was the same coming down and he applied this to his golf swing

Figure 3: Rotational Balance

especially in its downswing motion, where he didn't use applied force but relied on other forces already working in the swing: momentum and centrifugal force. (More on this later in the text).

So there are some basic laws of physics and how things interact that must be grasped. I have tried to simplify them here to create a better understanding of how these forces apply in the golf swing. I have named them, collectively, *Rotational Balance*, to get the concept more clearly across.

Definitions of key terms in the Perfect Balance program

The following terms are used throughout this text and apply to the golf swing. Understanding them well will assist you in duplicating the theories and allow you to increase your ability to improve your golf swing.

Balance: a system of distributing and regulating the shift of weight of the body in a physical activity such as golf or other rotational motion sports.

Dynamic: Relating to energy or physical force in motion, as opposed to STATIC. A force producing motion or change.

Motion: The action or process of change of position.

Kinetic: Of, relating to, or produced by motion.

Gravity: Force that tends to draw all bodies in the earth's sphere towards the center of the earth; in golf, that force which exerts resistance to the swinging club in the backswing and accelerates the club in the downswing.

Centrifugal force: The force tending to pull a thing outward when it is rotating rapidly around a center. In golf, the tendency of the swinging club head to pull away from the body in the forward swing as the rotation of the left arm and body direct the motion into a straight line at the ball.

Swing center: The action of moving or rotating the body from its center point or hub (breastbone or sternum) and maintaining a pivoting action in the golf swing.

Center of balance: the action of rotating the lower body between the arch and balls of the feet and maintaining an axis point in the classic and modern golf swing forms.

Rotational balance: The ability to regulate and control the swinging motion of the golf club in relation to the movement of the body in the golf swing action.

These are key terms to know in order to understand the action of the golf swing, the club head, and the role of dynamic motion and force in the swing.

The golf swing is a dynamic motion involving the laws of gravity and centrifugal force. If the student understands these aspects of the golf swing, he will improve his skill and mastery of the golf swing motion.

Master Swing Key: The keyword is Balance in the golf swing and is Golf's new motto of instruction: IMPROVE YOUR BALANCE, IMPROVE YOUR SWING AND YOUR GAME! Your Swing Key is Balance!

Chapter II

The Key Axioms of Perfect Balance in Golf Technique

Here then are the key principles of an effective golf swing, based on countless hours of study and observation. These concepts were developed over a period of twenty-five years, teaching and studying the swings of golfers — ranging from beginners to advanced players and professionals — and observing what actually works. They are presented here for your inspection and use as a set of fundamental axioms relating to an effective golf swing.

I have developed a new program based on these principles: *Perfect Balance: Your Key to Consistency and Shot-making in Golf*. This program includes a unique set of *balance awareness drills* formulated to help you improve your golf game, as well as other sports involving rotational balance. They are based on proven truths of the golf swing motion. In addition to this, you will learn about the recent discovery of the "balance principle of golf" and how it will transform your game to new heights and better scores.

> *Axiom 1: The primary factor in the golf swing is to swing the club (and body) in balance! The club and body are swung together in harmonious motion.*

> *Axiom 2: Balance is the cornerstone of the golf swing motion. From start to completion, control of the swing depends upon balance. This holds true for all rotational sports that use a club, bat, stick or racquet.*

> *Axiom 3: The action of the golf swing is to swing the club and body in rotational, balanced motion.*

> *Axiom 4: The common denominator to the golf swing motion is rotation. By that we mean rotating or swinging the weight of the club head in relation to the body and its center of balance through space.*

Axiom 5: Balance in the golf swing is the sensory or "feeling" mechanism that locates one's swing motion in and through space in hitting the ball.

Axiom 6: In the golf swing, maintaining balanced or stabilized motion around a fixed center point is the key to shot making and consistency. This holds true in all other rotational sports.

Axiom 7: The rotational formula consists of balance, swing tempo (speed) and rhythm in the golf swing motion.

Axiom 8: There are three primary actions in the golf swing motion that are interactive. These are planting, pivoting and driving. They are interdependent with one another in function. This relationship expands as each part is strengthened.

Axiom 9: Foot work and leg drive are the key essential balance points in the lower body platform in maintaining acceleration at the ball during the golf swing motion.

Axiom 10: All well executed golf shots are the result of swinging in dynamic and perfect balance from start to completion in the golf swing motion.

There are more than twenty axioms and principles that make up the Perfect Balance golf program, designed to increase your awareness and skill level in the area of balance and feel and shot-making. This book covers the basic axioms that form the foundation of this work.

As you progress through the material you will find newly discovered principles and information on the role of balance in golf and in sports motion generally—information never seen before in the sports world—that you can apply to improve your game.

It is my belief that you can be a better golfer and can easily improve both your game and your scoring potential. This book is dedicated to you and your improvement! May your game be the best it can be. Golf is the greatest of rotational sports and its mastery is a worthy adventure!

(Author's Note: These principles and axioms were formulated in the summer of 2005 for all golfers and instructors to use to improve the game of golf and enjoyment of the game, and to establish and codify, worldwide, a workable system of laws having to do with sports motion and balance in rotational sports.)

Chapter III

The Golf Instructional Model Has a Serious Flaw

Golfers all agree scores are too high

THE NATIONAL AVERAGE for 18 holes of golf is close to 103 for men and 108 for women. I think that is way too high. I think you agree! This is despite innovations in club and ball design that make the ball easier to hit. You can't tell me the game is so difficult that 95% of all golfers will never truly enjoy a round of golf. The average golfer with decent athletic skills should be able to shoot in the low 90 to 100 range without straining.

This average has not had a significant change in the last 50 years (for the record, an actual 0.9 strokes). That blows my mind a bit. I'll repeat: *the national average of 103 for men and 108 for women has improved by less than one stroke despite all the great new equipment we have.*

Wow! Something must be wrong with golf instruction.

The present instructional model has failed us

The advanced golfer performs his shot with *better balance* and *more consistent tempo* than the golfer who can't break 100. We all observed this—golfers and teachers alike—but failed to look any closer. It was one of those assumptions that we all made when we saw it done correctly: good golfers have excellent balance and poor golfers have poor balance and are inconsistent.

As a teacher of the game, I hear the constant complaint: "I want to improve consistency. I'm inconsistent in hitting the ball." It has a particularly discouraging ring to it, which led me to view it as a basic problem that needed investigating.

In our research, and especially our "Effortless Power" Workshops, we found that the advanced golfer has better balance and footwork and ability to maintain a consistent swing tempo, so he can release the club better at the ball. This is most notable in the role of lower body drive and footwork, but it had not previously been correlated to the golf swing. Even great teachers of the game did not know the real role of balance and footwork, although a few of the great players knew.

An evaluation of importances and a sort-out of what works and doesn't holds the key. What really helps golfers play better?

Various golf systems and theories abound. Most are geared to the way that instructors and players learned to play in their day, according to whatever theory was popular at the time.

Investigating the problem further

Two recent studies from golf swing motion analysis (utilizing reflective-dot computer technology and high speed videos to break down the swings of pro golfers), gave us a crucial look at the role of the club and body working together instant by instant in the golf swing.

Motion analysis is a relatively new field that studies motion by combining high speed video recording with computer imaging to create a detailed 3-dimensional view of an athlete in action. It is ideal for detailed analysis of performance, because a coach can take a movement apart frame by frame to see exactly what is happening.

I began this research work in earnest in the 2002 golf season, with an associate of mine and fellow golfer, John Massey. John is a computer training specialist.

I asked John to work with me and help head up a new study of the golf swing to debunk the belief that golf as a game is too difficult to master. Our first goal was a simplified approach to teaching golf to make it more enjoyable. It would be a bonus to lower scores as well. There were too many frustrated golfers in both our parts of town.

We both looked long and hard at the reasons the golf swing is difficult to master for so many golfers. Many hours were devoted to viewing the swings of advanced golfers, especially the pros.

We found quite a disparity between what the pros were doing and what the amateurs did. This was most noticeable in the ability to rotate and turn properly, dropping the club down and releasing the club and its energy right before impact.

With John's ability to isolate and evaluate problematic areas and keen computer skills, we spent many hours dissecting the pros and advanced players' golf swings, looking for the real errors in "real time".

By breaking down the golf swing into segments, frame by frame, we could see and isolate errors more easily. We could see that the swing errors were occurring in particular areas, especially the move away from the ball (Swing Position 1) and in the takeaway from the ball to waist-high (Swing Position 2). As a bonus, we could now see the early warning signs of larger problems, and red-flag them as they occurred.

The pros made swings with the driver at average speeds of 108–115 mph and were *on balance* almost every time with great tempo. The results were not surprising: they hit it long with pretty good accuracy. Tiger Woods was an exception, swinging the club head at an amazing 131 mph with the driver. Ernie Els swings at around 118 mph.

So the intriguing and driving QUESTION became: "How do you swing like that at such high speed, maintain uniform balance in the golf swing *and* do it effortlessly and consistently? "

Effective research consists of first identifying the problem areas and then narrowing the focus by analyzing the factors related to it. By discovering what works and what doesn't, we can isolate a reason (or reasons) for the problem and develop a workable solution.

The missing ingredient in golf instruction

The biggest difference between the advanced player and the average golfer was *balance*. We eventually discovered a missing factor in virtually all modern golf instruction. To me it looked like—and it eventually proved to be—the key missing factor: the teaching of BALANCE. That principle has taken a back seat to other, less useful teaching methodologies.

One clue was this observation that the majority of swing errors occurred in the *first two to three feet of the golf swing in the takeaway from the ball.*

As a matter of fact, about 75–80% of swing errors could be found in this takeaway area! Golfers out of balance had a faulty pattern from the beginning of their golf swings.

This basic fact was not something new to many instructors, who had been observing this phenomenon for years. Touring pros and advanced players echoed this sentiment about their own takeaway moves. They constantly check or monitor this move away from the ball. (Swing position 1—more on this later in the book.)

While it may not be a new observation, exactly how to correct it is a challenge that teaching pros have not been able to solve reliably. Golf instructors are good at diagnosing what is wrong; correcting it is another matter.

This problem has persisted for many years in golf instructional circles. For lack of a solution, too many golfers quit in frustration or never reach their full potential.

Unresolved problems such as this may very well have created the entire off-the-course golf school business, with its concentration on isolating a golfer's faults and correcting them with in-depth video analysis and tailored swing drills. Yet they, too, tend to teach too mechanical an approach.

These faults often showed up as a combination of errors—not as one primary swing fundamental. When this happened, the swing went drastically off the performance charts of the golfer: he would hit the ball poorly and inconsistently. It was almost like looking at an entirely different golfer during the times when he had two or three swing errors working simultaneously in the takeaway, compared with times when he hit the swing positions and patterns correctly.

When one of these swing error combinations was made (a reverse pivot, straightening the right or back leg, over rotating the foot or ankle, etc.), the golfer would not perform well and would sense that his "golf swing was off." Worse, it would *stay* off. Often, the harder the golfer tried to fix it, the worse the problem became.

I call this phenomenon, the *click effect:* a golfer will inadvertently revert to the incorrect form and thereafter get stuck in a wrong swing move or feel, caught up in swing mechanics, and upset no end with his score for the day.

Most golfers with higher handicaps (i.e., the majority of golfers) manifest a pattern or combination of swing errors, especially in the *initial or first phase* of both the back swing and the downswing movement. The more compensation there is in these key areas, the more inconsistency the golfer has in his or her shots.

In my investigation I began to think that this situation must have something to do with *readjusting* or *compensating* their balance, or even not knowing how to *find* their balance or feel of the swing's motion in the first place. Could there be a missing link or key basic that was not being taught in the golf swing? Did modern golf swing instruction, with its emphasis on generating power, overlook a key fundamental?

So my golf school staff and I decided to look at this from all angles. In doing so, we knew that we would have to examine what was actually being taught to the golfer, and examine more closely our golf fundamentals.

Chapter IV

Golfers Don't Understand Key Fundamentals in the Golf Swing

I DISCOVERED THAT golfers scored very poorly on tests of golf fundamentals, and that the role of balance, pivot and the swing plane were grossly misunderstood. Student understanding of these key actions in the golf swing was visibly missing in swing application.

A classic example of this was the student (who had been playing for years) who thought "pivot" had to do with *twisting* the body, rather than *turning* or coiling. In another case, a pro golfer I was working with didn't know what "flex" meant when asked to "put more flex in the knees and legs" in her set-up and swing.

In further examining this notion that there was a primary error in the golf swing motion, I discovered that *there was a more basic error previously not seen in the takeaway* from the ball. It may have been suspected, but could not be seen by the naked eye by instructors.

The real error in the swing

Although high speed camera and swing analysis can see with great detail, instructors have been looking at *the point of impact* in the golf swing for the answer. It was never suspected until now that the real error in the swing was in the takeaway with the golfer's *balance: his deviation from his swing center point!* In other words, instructors and their students have been looking for the problem in the wrong area.

What the golfer does at impact position in the downswing is the cumulative result of factors that occur much earlier in the swing: how he initiates the backswing, keeps balanced, and pivots in his swing motion. The pros instinctively know this. They make an effective pivot and rotation to swing the club and they maintain their balance throughout the swing.

The problem is in the *degree of deviation from the golfer's center of balance.* This is controlled by the amount of coil the golfer makes with his lower body in the backswing motion, especially the pelvis and hip area.

Over-rotation in the backswing and initial takeaway from the ball is the problem. If you start your swing with a move or thrust of the hips going back (as you may have been taught to do), you are *already out of position and off balance.* In the downswing you will be trying to compensate with the club and body to get in balance and back on swing path.

Furthermore, in an effort to gain power, many students rotate the lower body too quickly in the backswing with the hips and knees, instantly throwing off their balance and timing. This causes a host of backswing errors. Keep in mind that 80% of all golf swing errors are in the backswing.

Golfers who do this have to create various forms of compensation with their arms and bodies to recover their balance point, all in a quick instant before hitting the ball. (The entire golf swing motion for a fast swing is a little more than a second, barely two seconds even for a slower swing. Both swings are effective if they are done correctly; the key is to maintain balance throughout the swing motion.)

Good balance comes from better footwork, from making an effective pivot in the golf swing in the correct sequence, and from learning the correct timing pattern—tempo and rhythm. (More on this in detail as we go through the book).

In studying swing patterns, we found that much of the problem arose from a faulty setup position where the weight placed on the feet was *off balance* to start with.

This error causes the student to lose the neutral position of foot integration with the lower body. He or she is then forced to create a counterbalance effect very early in the swing. (Getting the weight centered on the back foot and inner right thigh area creates a neutral position for the foot. This is one of the keys to a correct swing.)

The error continues from the top of the backswing in the first downswing motion to the ball, the golfer fighting this out-of-balance state as he tries to make a quick compensatory move towards the ball with his body or hands and by altering the speed of his swing (speeding up).

The important errors in initial swing motion, alone or in combination, can be categorized as follows:

- Weight back on heels

- Weight concentrated or centered on forefoot or toes

- Weight on heels and to the right

- Weight too far forward on toes

- Weight back on heels and on left side

- Torso is too top heavy with weight leaning forwards towards the toes

- Over-rotation of ankles and knees in takeaway

- Lowering left shoulder at start of back swing

- Sweeping club inside quickly on back swing

- Left knee moving towards ball with right hip raised

- Spine angle deviated from

- Lack of control of club head and swing

- Swinging mainly with the arms and not the body

The ideal position is the weight distributed evenly to the inside of each foot, with 55% of the weight in the forefoot and 45% of the weight in the heel to middle part of the foot.

Legendary Sam Snead said this: *"Balance is important in any golf shot and so in taking up your stance your weight should be evenly balanced between both*

Figure 1: *Swing Position 0 — Set Up at Address. Weight centered between the feet.*

feet, and in each foot evenly balanced between the ball and heel of the foot."
"Natural Golf", by Sam Snead, p. 33.

From my research a few years back with Dr. Jeff Blanchard, a leading chiropractic sports physician and pro golfer, and current research with Doctors Stuart Steinberg and Kylie Zani, podiatrists, I saw that a golfer's weight distribution tended to "list"—lean one way more than the other—sideways, from back to front, or a combination of both.

When the golfer performed our "eyes closed" test, he tended to lean in a particular direction in an effort to counterbalance his position, seeking to get his feet in what we call the "neutral position" in preparation for the swing. Interestingly enough, 50–60% of all golfers studied had improper balance at set-up position to the ball.

In watching footage of tour players, we observed players establishing this set position, setting proper balance and alignment. We watched Tiger Woods, Ernie Els, Nick Faldo, Greg Norman and Jack Nicklaus in their set up routines all getting the body, via the feet and legs, in an optimum neutral position to start the swing.

So the problem we see here is that golfers don't have a built-in reference point in relation to their balance and are not taught to think *balance* and *feel* in the current instructional model. They are taught to think *mechanics* instead, and cannot effectively locate their balance points — especially their swing's center point — as they swing back, down and through.

Getting footwork and timing working together is vital to dynamic balance in the swing, and crucial to a successful repetitive swing motion. Talk to any advanced player and you will find that *footwork is the key* to the all important lower body move during the golf swing, providing the rhythm and the sensory "beat to the music."

Chapter V

Investigating the Golf Instructional Swing Model

THE MOST PREVALENT schools of thought placed importance on the "swing plane." In doing so, they produced a very mechanical model of instruction and mind-set for golfers and students to try to replicate. The result of this approach was a large group of golfers who were too mechanical in approach to their golf swings and subsequently did not reach their potential.

In the late 1940s and into the 1950s, we saw the emergence of a swing style made popular by the great player Ben Hogan, who kept the left heel down almost completely in the backswing and made reference to his famous "pane of glass" swing plane dimension in his book, *The Five Fundamentals of Golf*.

Everyone who played golf wanted to, and occasionally did, emulate Hogan's flatter swing plane, keeping the left heel down more in the backswing. The hottest catchword in golf throughout the country at the time — with golfers and especially instructors — was "swing plane." His swing style was in opposition to the classic golf swing of the day.

Unfortunately, many golfers who took up the game over the years who had read Hogan's book as their first golf primer carried the concept of "swing plane" forward in their games. Yet very few golf students could define, far less demonstrate, what "swing plane" really meant.

Additionally, instruction was going "modern", not only preaching "swing plane," but introducing a new series of "important body positions" and additional swing mechanics to keep in mind during the golf swing.

The "swing plane" theory also made things more difficult for many players as they got older, because it requires using the spine as the primary pivot point, instead of the right knee and leg.

Realistically, the concept of the swing plane was too technically difficult for most golfers to perform easily in their swings, let alone to truly understand. This created a tremendous gap in their understanding of golf basics.

The term "swing plane" turned out to be, from my personal surveys with hundreds of golfers as well as surveys at our golf schools, the most misunderstood term among students of the game. (Swing plane, balance and pivot were found to be the three major areas of misunderstanding in the golf swing.)

This non-comprehension carried through to the instructional ranks as well, with teachers having their varied opinions about the technical aspects of being "on- and off-plane" in the swing and follow-through.

During a national teaching "summit" in 1950 by the PGA of America, it is said that Hall of Fame golfer Bobby Jones, winner of the Grand Slam of Golf, recommended a teaching method made popular by Ernest Jones for its effectiveness and simplicity. However, it was not embraced by the board of directors for *fear of teaching fewer lessons* to students. (Ernest Jones had *more of his students win national amateur and open championships* than any other golf instructor in the history of the game, and a high level of success with thousands of students who praised his effective methods.)

"Just swinging the club head" was not *complicated* enough, and as a result lost its importance and was "politely" moved to the back of the teaching bus. Swinging or hitting for accuracy off the tee also seemed take a back seat during this period.

Golf instruction got out of touch with its simplicity. Great teachers of the game and their legacies from the "golden age of golf" created by Bobby Jones, Walter Hagen, and Gene Sarazen—greats such as Ernest Jones, Percy Boomer, Henry Cotton and Tommy Armour—were almost forgotten.

Golf swing instruction became complicated, and this viewpoint was carried forward by teachers who made their living from giving lessons. It also became difficult and ineffective, no matter the attractions of the "swing plane is king" theory.

Emphasis today is placed on using the larger muscles of the upper body region in the golf swing, creating rotation of the left shoulder and arm away from the body and restricting hip turn by keeping the left heel down as the club is swung to the top of the backswing. The spine, or a point to the right of the spine, is the pivot point employed in this system.

Present day instruction uses a mechanical model of the golf swing involving emphasis on static swing positions: a succession of body, arm and hand positions encased in a "muscle memory pattern." The idea is to swing the club on the swing plane back and through, to achieve club head speed. New equipment, especially lighter graphite shafts and light weight metal woods, encourages such swinging of the club.

Advanced golfers and top pros gravitated towards this swing method and in doing so, the era of "hitting it hard" with bigger swing speeds and the newer equipment and ball evolved. The era of the "power game" had emerged.

Modern professional golfers, better athletes in general than their predecessors, who *can* produce a strong athletic move and have the flexibility to keep the left heel down in the golf swing, are the most successful with this swing philosophy. The majority of these golfers were indoctrinated in this mechanical model of golf instruction.

Equipment got better, but scores didn't

This era of the "modern" golf swing also saw the ushering in of new space age materials: titanium driver faces and graphite shafts. We got bigger club heads with deeper faces, and clubs made more "forgiving" to offset poorly centered hits. Yet for all this high technology, scores for the average golfer didn't improve. Why?

Unfortunately, although length off the tee improved, golfers were now hitting less *accurately* off the tee. Inconsistency in their swings negated any outright gain in distance. Golfers were hitting into trouble in the rough and behind trees more often, so overall scores did not really improve.

The emphasis on "Drive for show and putt for dough" was nice in theory but unrealistic in practice, mainly because golfers were trying to consciously hit for power rather than produce an *effortless* power in the timing and pace of their swings. Good control and "feeling" the swing in motion was overshadowed by the claims of golf club manufacturers, advertising improved power and added distance.

That is the liability with this method: it encourages the student to "hit it hard" and go too much for distance.

The "take control of the swing with the large muscles of the torso" golf philosophy widened the gap between the advanced and the average golfer who was still trying to break the 90–100 score barrier.

Advanced and professional players, being more athletic, could successfully perform the big swing with the new technology. The average golfer, lacking the strength and flexibility, produced off center hits with erratic club head speed and lack of control.

During this era, an avalanche of books stressed mechanics and swing positions one must develop. These helped to set the mechanical swing philosophy in concrete.

The terms "balance" and "feel" in golf books written during this time lost their importance. An actual description, or even use of the word "balance" itself in golf texts, was hard to find. Even if it were found, it lacked essential detail.

By the early 1950s, then, a new era in golf had emerged with an emphasis on "modern swing mechanics." It was fueled in particular by instructors who themselves had been schooled in these principles. The "power game" enjoyed dominance in the golf arena for the next 50+ years.

Regardless of technological advances in club and ball design, the national average has not risen more than one stroke in 60 years. So the question to ask is: If there has been no real change in the ability to play better golf and improve golf scores, doesn't it stand to reason that there is a fundamental error or a hidden influence that has not been identified?

The "Classic" swing

Ernest Jones, Percy Boomer, Tommy Armour, Harvey Pennick, Bob Toski and a few others continued to "keep the torch alive" by keeping the golf swing pure and simple in their golf instruction, but it was the great Sam Snead, with his wonderfully smooth swing and tempo, who became golf's greatest ambassador.

Fifty years later Snead continued to preach the importance of swinging the club head and creating rhythm and timing in the swing motion, putting our attention on the true importances. He admonished us for "thinking too much" about the swing instead of getting into action, getting lost in the mechanics and out of touch with balance and swing motion as one in the golf swing. Snead personified simplicity of power and natural movement in the golf swing.

> *Axiom 14: The primary action of the golf swing is held to be: Swing the club in balance! Balance and swing motion act together interdependently.*

The top instructors in the past taught swinging the golf club in the classic golf swing style, where the left arm rotated across the torso with the left heel coming off the ground and with more hip and pelvic rotation to help get the club rotated to the top. A strong robust rotation of the left shoulder and hip were emphasized with the hands high above the ears in the backswing move.

Although this classic swing style developed out of the equipment of its day, before steel shafts and with hickory wood golf shafts, much of the "swing the club" philosophy was present and was a significant part of this proven and effective method.

The *key move* in the forward swing to the target was getting *the left heel down quickly* and rotating the lower body, especially the legs and thighs, into hitting up against the left side, inner left thigh and knee position at impact. No golfer made this move better than golfing greats Bobby Jones, Tom Watson and especially Jack Nicklaus. (We can't forget the classic swing of Payne Stewart winning the US Open at Pinehurst).

Heavy emphasis on the "swing plane" principle was not part of this classic style of golf swing instruction. Using balance, especially with footwork and "feeling" the club head being swung around the body, was the emphasis.

I would like to coin a new term that places emphasis on balance in the golf swing motion: *Rotational Balance.* I chose this because it stresses the importance of rotation in the golf swing. It is this specialized definition of balance we will be working with here in this work and some of its drills.

> *Sam Snead:* "*Balance is important in any golf shot and so in taking up your stance your weight should be evenly balanced between both feet, and in each foot evenly balanced between the ball and heel of the foot...*" Natural Golf, Sam Snead, p. 33.

> *Master Golf Tip:* *Find your balance or 'balance point' in your set-up. You find your balance point this way: Stand up to the ball and go into your set-up position. Let your hands hang down forming a triangle. Move your weight forward towards your toes and rock back towards your heels. It's natural for your balance to settle towards the middle part of the foot. Your weight should be centered more towards the middle and ball of the foot region and arch of both the left and right foot. You should feel athletic and ready for action in the golf swing. When you have an athletic set-up that feels stable in its base with the lower body, and feels comfortable, and when your weight feels centered over feet, you have located your balance point in the set-up and are "good to go." You can practice this with and without the club.*

Summary

We can see that golf instruction evolved to a point where fundamentals were relegated to lesser importance, even neglected. They were replaced by "advanced" principles emphasizing technical and mechanical aspects of the swing. In doing so, instruction has lost the essence of the golf swing and its teaching, which is based on FEEL and the natural laws of motion.

Due to this evolution away from these key fundamentals, golf instructors today are teaching a mechanical golf model that is too difficult for the average golfer to learn, giving them the feeling that they cannot master the game, or that it is too frustrating and not worth the effort.

Rotational Balance must become the new catch-phrase of golf and the instructional world. The golf world needs more simplicity.

Chapter VI

Why Are Golfers Failing to Learn the Game?

THERE ARE MANY fine instructors of the game. (This work is also dedicated to them.) These teachers keep instruction simple, emphasize swinging the club in motion and adherence to the basics.

Yet much of golf instruction has merely picked up the latest theory or some tour player's success, touted by the popular golf magazines, with his swing gracing the cover and his technique the subject of its lead article.

Instruction has continued to stress the principle of the swing plane as the key to a student's understanding of the golf swing. As we saw, this principle has not been well understood by students of the game. The average golfer wants to play his best without having to become a serious athlete, and so "swing plane" instruction has not produced results.

How could one understand, grasp and apply the concept of the swing plane if he did not know an earlier key step, a primary fundamental: the role of balance?

Straightening out the confusion

Golf instruction can be confusing. Teaching programs differ, and in some cases teach completely different philosophies of the swing and various key points of technique. Student confusion is a recognized problem and golfers aren't improving very much. Sometimes they are worsening.

For fifty years or more, equipment has gotten better and better. Better equipment should create more golfers and better scores. But that is not what happens in practice.

What does the advanced golfer do that the inexperienced golfer doesn't do?

Top golfers have impeccable balance and poor players have poor balance: that was the basic factor we discovered. Golfers I have taught, however, from beginner to advanced, aren't necessarily aware of this at first. What they all want to improve is just one thing: their consistency.

What they discover is that they are inconsistent in their ball striking *because they fall off balance or out of balance* frequently in hitting their shots.

The primary factors differentiating Better Players from Poor Players are:

- Good or Poor Balance
- Effective or Ineffective Pivoting
- Consistency or Inconsistency
- In Control or Out of Control
- Good or Poor Timing
- Better swing path or plane

Why the existing instructional model is ineffective

Imagine trying to learn a sport such as judo or fencing where you were taught only the sophisticated moves that advanced students, who had been working on their form for years, were expected to perform: techniques almost impossible to execute without thorough knowledge of the simple basics of the sport.

Would you enjoy it? Would you feel like you were learning, or would you become frustrated and discouraged?—Of course you would! That's exactly what happens to most people when they start to learn golf.

The student is in over his head, usually in the first golf lesson, with a series of terms he doesn't understand and actions he can't grasp, far less demonstrate to the instructor. The learning gradient is too steep for him to attain understanding and an ability to perform the actions. All too often, he never does grasp these basics, and quits after a few months or years.

In the existing teaching model, instructors theorise too much about the technical actions of the swing instead of teaching its simplicity of motion. Instead, they teach swing theory and swing actions that are too complicated for beginning or even intermediate golfers.

The golf swing is not broken down by the majority of instructors into basic actions for the beginner and intermediate student first, with precise definitions of key terms at each point. There is no demonstration by the student back to the instructor of each defined action, so that instructors can see what the student understands and can demonstrate.

Our current instructional model is too one-sided. The instructor focuses on the theory of the swing and doesn't bring enough student drilling and practice into the instruction.

Really checking with the student on each key part, to consult his understanding and ability to apply principles, is also missing.

Such instructional actions are necessary in building the golf swing from (quite literally) the ground up, beginning with the basics of stance, alignment to the ball, and grip.

The golf lesson is for the *student*, not the instructor, and it is the responsibility of the instructor to build up the student's confidence with actions he can perform and to get the student winning on each level before going on to the next. The goal is that the student not only understands the basic theory of the golf swing but can apply it in his or her own swing.

Putting the right pieces together in learning the golf swing

So what we have had is a teaching methodology that is focused on telling students what they are doing wrong, instead of teaching them how to do it right. Correct instruction starts from the very basics, drilling each part to a win, allowing the student to build his golf swing on a progressive series of successes.

The sequence in which the information is presented and the identification of the key principles are both vitally important in order for the student to gain understanding of the golf swing and to develop his ability to apply.

When the instructor finds, through regular checking, that the student has difficulty in application, it is his job to find out what's been missed in previous actions and get the student to review and drill those to better skill. The student can then move forward successfully.

The pieces are in front of us, we need just *to assemble them in their correct order and importance* and in doing so reshape and design the true working model of golf's instructional basics. A sturdy house always begins with a sound foundation.

This book provides the essential foundation which had almost disappeared and places it back into golf instruction where it belongs.

The primary fundamental on which the golf swing depends is **balance.** All other fundamentals depend on this one factor. This has indeed been a piece of lost technology that has now been brought back to the party as the main attraction. As the invited guest, you are cordially invited to join the fun.

In *The Ultimate Game of Golf,* which I wrote in 1993, I referred to *"balance as the cornerstone or chief fundamental in the golf swing,"* yet even I had not realized the importance of this statement at the time. As I continued to train students and instructors and evaluated the problems and frustrations that they experienced, I began to see how integral a factor *balance* truly was in attaining consistency. What I had found true in 1993 is even more so today, and has been true since the earliest days of golf.

Sports motion golf study reveals key information

In the fall of 2004, I began to formulate some theories about the key role of movement and swing motion, especially balance, in sports like golf. This was after a significant amount of time observing students and evaluating

Motion Analysis using Reflective Dot Technology

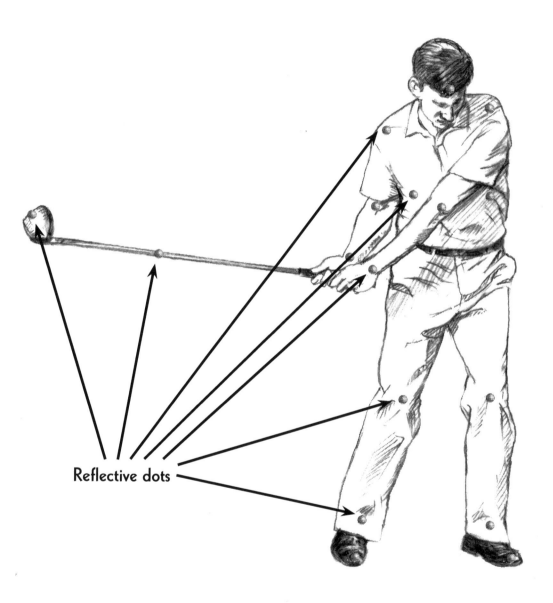

Reflective dots

Figure 1: Reflective dot sensors on golfer's body and golf club allow computer-analysis of the swing. (Shown: swinging toward impact.)

the factors that made our teaching methods successful as well as researching additional data on the subject.

I accepted an invitation to visit one of the leading U.S. biomechanics labs, the Human Performance and Biomechanics lab at Children's Hospital of San Diego, California, where human motion and performance are studied. During my visit, I identified additional factors relating to balance and movement that provided more pieces to the puzzle of "what was the underlying cause of all these swing errors?" I met with Arnel Aguinlado, the director of the lab, who has worked with numerous professional baseball pitchers and other athletes isolate biomechanical weaknesses in their pitching technique and performance.

After setting up a testing module using specific parameters relating to the factors I wanted to study in the golf swing motion—lower body movement and especially footwork—we began our research into the dynamics of golf swing motion. Not only was this a "real time" environment, with myself and other golfers joining in the testing module, but we also utilized a 3-D computer model of the golf swing motion using reflective-dot technology sensors. This technology creates a full omni-directional look at the golf swing and it showed us things you normally can't see using video alone.

It was from this work on special swing motion studies, comparing the range of motion and rotation of the top pros with that of average golfers, that the truth of the golf swing motion became very clear. It allowed us to isolate the most fundamental aspects of the golf swing: balance, hand action, swing plane and timing, with balance leading the way.

What the computer model showed us was a revelation: *the primary motion in the golf swing starts with the ball of the foot and arch area in its rotation from the front to back foot and side to side motion.* This supports the classic principle that the motion starts from the ground up.

From this initial movement, the entire swing is set in motion from the left foot as the weight shifts to the back foot. The legs, shoulders and hips pick up the lead of the movement, creating a coiling effect around the back right leg and hip. The concentration of weight shifts from the ball of the foot progressively back toward the heel when using the longer clubs, especially the woods and driver.

Chapter VII

Developing an Effective Instructional Model

The swings of advanced players and pros

THE COMMON DENOMINATOR that produced consistency in the swings and ball striking of advanced and pro golfers was that they had mastered the flow from static to dynamic balance in their golf swings. Balance, rotation and timing were under their control.

Master Golf Swing Tip: The golf swing is a movement controlled by balance. The name of the game in swinging "in perfect balance" like the pros is Rotational Balance. Placing one's attention and awareness on this true basic opens the door to consistency and shot-making.

Building an effective instructional model

We reviewed and analyzed numerous instructional models. Only one or two teaching systems came close to what we were looking for in our analysis.

In examining golf instructors who had routinely gotten the best results and had the most champion players, two names emerged. In the modern era of golf instruction, their names do not make the top ten and they are not significantly noted for their contributions, yet their material is used even today without full credit.

Jack Nicklaus is considered the greatest golfer of the twentieth century. But in golf *instruction* that accolade belongs to Ernest Jones: the top golf instructor of the last 100 years. His name ranks with Percy Boomer, Stewart Maiden (whose brother taught Bobby Jones), Henry Cotton and Tommy Armour. These dedicated teachers shaped the game of golf through their successful teaching methods and represent the "golden age of golf instruction" from 1920-1950. To these men I dedicate this book.

Ernest Jones' brilliant and effective work (*Swing the Club Head*, 1937) stresses the fundamentals of gravity and centrifugal force in the golf swing and its motion. It provides a method to exercise swing motion and develop feel, and to get the golf student to do it. It is also one of the first applications of physics to the golf swing motion that I know of.

This method became the working model to emulate, and to derive our motion analysis studies from in our modern rendition of the "kinetic motion chain" of the club and body in the golf swing. Ernest Jones' contribution to golf highlighted the fundamentals of motion and the force of gravity.

Henry Cotton's work, as written in his book *The Game of Golf* (1948), concurs with Ernest Jones' philosophy and is legendary in teaching circles, especially in Europe.

Percy Boomer, author of the book *On Learning to Play Better Golf*, is another noted teacher from this era. He helped shape the fundamentals of modern day instruction. His work contributed to the modern swing theories of top teachers such as David Leadbetter, Butch Harmon, Jim Flick, Jim McLean and a few others, including myself.

Boomer, like Ernest Jones, also emphasized the role of swinging the club head, not hitting hard or using force itself as a component. He was a proponent of using the natural laws of movement, especially rhythm and timing as a flowing motion. His success with students centered on rhythm as a key fundamental in the golf swing.

Ernest Jones, Percy Boomer, Tommy Armour, Stewart Maiden and the other great teachers of golf's golden era, emphasized the true fundamentals, especially balance and timing as the key elements in the golf swing.

Modern instructors who influence golf swing instruction, like David Leadbetter and Butch Harmon, have done a good job of building the components of the physical model and relating the role of timing and tempo in the golf swing. Their emphasis, however, is on a more *mechanical* definition and application of the golf swing. All of these systems tend to minimize the primary role of balance and motion as one in the golf swing.

Most of these systems make the assumption that balance is a "given" and is achieved mainly by the athletic set-up, but there is more to it than that. Getting the swing "on plane" without knowing the role of balance is like trying to make eggs and bacon without knowing you're supposed to first crack the eggs.

No one truly had all the answers in this area of sports motion and performance. Important fundamentals got lost or neglected in the evolution to the modern swing. The factor of balance became relegated to "less important" status and we lost track of just how vital balance is to any true understanding of (or ability to execute) a successful, consistent golf swing.

Axiom 24: The foundation of swing fundamentals is built upon balance, with swing tempo and rhythm comprising the timing for-

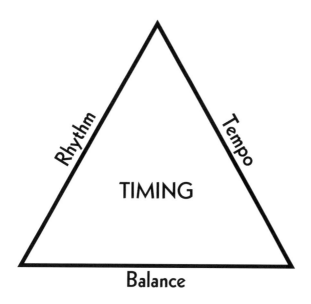

Figure 1: The Timing Formula in the Golf Swing

mula in the golf swing. Each is interdependent upon the others, with balance being the most important.

There are some outstanding instructors in the U.S. and the international scene in the world of golf. These very dedicated individuals get results that run far better than the national average. They work with junior golf programs and are what make the instructional field of golf an inspiration to all teachers.

In looking at their merits and what they do best, they are successful by their adherence to fundamentals and their inherent belief in balance and timing as the true fundamentals of the golf swing and they should be applauded. The best teachers are effective communicators, know their subject and are successful in teaching the fundamentals to their students.

As I said in the introduction to this book, you have a choice: to continue with the existing model emphasizing swing plane, technical swing positions and a multitude of mechanics (which produces a national average of over one hundred for men and women); or to create a higher potential of gain, understanding and enjoyment of the game by learning Rotational Balance in the new *Perfect Balance in the Golf Swing* method, based on natural laws and principles of motion.

Many golfers are experiencing great success with these principles. The demand for this "return to key basics" golf instructional program is getting stronger and stronger as golfers discover this is a system that gets results.

Chapter VIII

Developing an Instructional Model Based on Golf's Key Fundamental: Balance!

WE STARTED WITH a basic premise that there must be a missing key fundamental underlying the situation of so many golfers failing to achieve success and consistency in their game. We found that fundamentals such as balance and "feel" in hitting the ball had been replaced with more mechanistic ideas, such as technical swing positions and a fixation on the importance of the swing plane, along with the demand for technological advances in the area of golf equipment manufacturing.

I went back to my *Ultimate Game of Golf* book and reviewed that material for information on the golf swing. I picked up a clue in the area of "power" and its development in the swing. I had created a drill at the time to enhance this specific ability, but upon survey of students I found that there was some misunderstanding of the principles. I reworked the drill to clarify the concept of power and its relationship to the golf swing.

I then started delivering this information and the application of it in the form of a golf workshop, entitled "How to Harness Effortless Power in the Golf Swing."

The results were dramatic: one for one, students understood the formula for effortless power and the fundamentals behind it. They were able to demonstrate their understanding by hitting drives and fairway woods with less force and more graceful, rhythmic swings.

Although this change netted improvement for many, I continued to observe and hear complaints of inconsistency. It was one thing to hit a 275 yard drive down the fairway, but the fairways hit in regulation play still remained poor due to inconsistency in shot making. Inconsistency was prevalent in all key areas including greens hit in regulation, up and downs, and even putting.

Another clue emerged: It had not occurred to me prior to this point to examine the idea that balance *by itself* could be the primary fundamental, because I had always *assumed* it to be understood as such. I had written that balance was the cornerstone fundamental in my first book, *The Ultimate Game of Golf,* but had made the error of assuming that all golfers knew about balance and that it must be something else that plagued the player, most likely in the area of the mental game.

Restoring the factor of balance to its proper importance led to an improvement in its definition and how it related to rotation, the common denominator of the golf swing motion.

The forgotten factor of balance has been rediscovered and the intent of this book is to revitalize and reincorporate this factor to the golf swing instructional model to help players achieve consistency and enjoyment of the game. Imagine experiencing the flowing swings, the skills and grace of golf's golden age performers: Vardon, Jones, Hagen, Nelson, Snead and Hogan, Palmer, Nicklaus and Player, Casper, Watson and Trevino. Now, wouldn't that revitalize your interest and enjoyment of the game?

Golf balance and motion test

Here's the complete balance and motion test I've developed for golfers, with the help of an experienced sports physician, that will help you to identify key aspects relating to your consistency, balance, timing and hitting.

This test will increase your awareness of how your balance (or lack of it) is affecting your golf swing.

Golf balance and motion questionnaire

On a scale of 1 to 5, (1 being lowest and 5 highest) rank yourself on the following points in relation to your balance in the golf swing.

1. How do you rate yourself on balance in general? Not only in golf but in life and sports.

2. Do you tend to lose your balance in your golf swing, say in a particular direction, like backward, to the side or forwards or in some combination of the above?

3. Do you tend to hit the ball with most of your weight on your back leg on the forward swing to the target?

4. Do you feel, or have others told you, that you "hit from the top" or "come over the top" in your golf swing?

5. When taking the club back in your backswing, do you swing quickly to the inside with a relatively big hip turn?

6. In swinging the club back, do you find your weight stays too much or more on your left foot and side?

7. Do you turn or pivot around your left foot or ankle more than you should?

8. Do you shift your weight too quickly going back in your takeaway?

9. In your swing going back, does your left shoulder move downward towards the knee instead of coming back directly under the chin at the top of your backswing?

10. Do you tend to sway or move laterally with your lower body (hips) on the backswing?

11. In your downswing, do you have to quickly slide your lower body, especially the hips and legs, towards the ball and target?

12. Upon completing your swing, are you on balance and in a resting position or can't hold a balanced finish?

13. In your set-up to the ball, is your weight set up more towards your heels than on the ball of the foot arch region?

14. Is your weight more set towards your toes than on the arch and ball of the foot region of the foot?

15. Do you start your golf swing with a weight shifting action or the motion of the club head going back?

16. Is your weight at set-up evenly distributed or more on one leg than the other?

17. Do you try to over power your shots and try to hit it hard losing your balance?

18. How aware are you of using footwork in the hitting of your shots? (Very aware=5, Unaware=0)

19. In swinging back and through, how aware are you of the weight of the club head swinging around your body?

20. Do you tend to stand with your weight more to one side than the other while standing at rest or in the set-up position?

Total Score _____

85-100 Very Good

70-85 Good

55-70 Fair

40 -55 Poor

The purpose of the balance test is to give you, perhaps for the first time, a look at how you currently incorporate balance into your golf swing and how it may be affecting your consistency, swing and the key to better scores and mental game focus.

Instructors have been hearing it for some time:

"I'm inconsistent in my game."

"I want to be more consistent!"

"My tee shots miss the fairway and my irons are right and left of the green."

"I can't hit the ball with any real control or consistency with my swing."

"Even with all the new technological advances in club design and the golf ball, my shots and game is still too inconsistent and I have not improved in score."

The *apparent* reasons for inconsistency in the golf swing can be linked to a number of different areas (balance, swing path, pivot, and timing), but the real underlying *causes* of a lack of consistency are contained in this key discovery:

> *Inconsistency in golf is directly related to the amount of deviation from the golfer's center of balance and sense of timing of the arms and hands with rotation of the body. When the golfer is controlling his balance, he can maintain his center of gravity, balance and spine angle without effort. And, in doing so, hit more consistent golf shots.*

This is the key to understanding this book, and the most important fundamental in all of golf instruction.

You can spend years (maybe you already have!) worrying about spine angle, swing plane, muscle tension, and a hundred other mechanical aspects of your golf swing. THEY ALL RESOLVE without further attention when you concentrate on BALANCE and TIMING and get them right.

Chapter IX

Definition of Balance as it Pertains to Golf

BEFORE WE GO any further, I should define what balance is specifically as it pertains to the golf swing.

A survey of golfers in our research program found the following interesting facts:

- ❧ The majority couldn't provide an adequate definition of balance nor tell how it works, but did answer that a good shot was the result of better balance;

- ❧ Golfers said that they never considered using their feet more in the swing;

- ❧ In regards to balance, they did not know how to make a proper pivot, and could not define or demonstrate a correct coil or pivot;

- ❧ When asked to identify the source of power in the golf swing, they said it came mostly from the shoulders, legs and arms.

So I thought it would be a good idea to define what balance really is.

We'll start with the dictionary definition: Balance, as a noun, is "a state of equilibrium, steadiness." As a verb it means "to bring into or maintain in a state of equilibrium."

As it applies to golf and swinging the club, we need a specialized definition that is tested and effective. Here it is:

Definition: Balance in the golf swing is the sensory mechanism or "feel" that locates one's swing motion in and through space in hitting the ball. (This is Axiom 5 of the Perfect Balance in Golf program.)

In other words, Balance is the sensory awareness of maintaining the ever-changing swing center point in motion with movement of the body and club as one in a unit of motion. It is the regula-

tion of that perception in a timed, steadied pattern of motion. Balance, rhythm and timing act as one.

There are some points here that I want to emphasize strongly:

- ❧ The golfer learns to *control* this interaction, the timing of the club and balance of the body, as one unit.

- ❧ *This is an acquired skill* that can be isolated and practiced.

- ❧ It is *not* mysterious, or something only the "chosen few" can master.

In order to do this well, the golfer has only to learn to work from a base (the feet) and a movable platform (the lower body), and to sense the shift of his weight in relation to the rotation of the club head as he moves it around his body. Once that is mastered, he learns to be focused on the target at the same time.

He creates a state of equilibrium among the forces of motion and the movement of his body back and through the golf shot and heightens his intention to hit the shot to a given target as his main goal.

One improves his skill by mastering these key interactions. The swing pattern and movement of the club, which has weight to its motion, the pull of gravity and (especially) centrifugal force are all part of the synchronized, all-in-one action of the golf swing.

The golfer utilizes the swinging motion of the arms and hands along with the rotation of the bigger muscles of the torso as a working unit.

Balance in the golf swing is the sensory mechanism or "feel" that locates one's swing motion in and through space in hitting the ball.

Chapter X

The Discovery of the Balance Principle in Golf

A NEW SET of fundamentals has been developed based on the role of balance, "feel" and sports motion. These principles have been formulated into a series of unique drills to assist you in taking your game to the next level. We'll take a look at the "balance principles of golf" as our next step.

> *Axiom 11: The primary factor in all sports utilizing a club (golf), bat, racquet or stick is dynamic, balanced motion.*

> *Axiom 3: The action of the golf swing is to swing the club and body in a rotational, balanced motion.*

If you were taught the popular myths that "balance comes naturally" or that "you are either athletic or you're not," you may have decided that you'd never get really good at golf. The instruction and coaching of balance in golf has been mainly an assumption that golfers "knew" about balance without it being recognized as something that can be isolated and improved. Golfers learning the game had a key part missing that hurt the development of an effective golf swing.

We have returned to the key basics of the golf swing motion and have for the first time a balance system in golf—a series of simple but powerful balance awareness drills incorporated into golf instruction.

Studies conducted at our golf schools and feedback from our students show that improving balance in the golf swing (and so improving consistency) just by 5–10% can improve one's shot-making and scores by 3–5 strokes. A 10–25 % improvement in balance can produce a 5–9 stroke improvement.

When a golfer masters his balance in the golf swing, his shot-making can improve his scores as much as 10–15 strokes, depending on his handicap and experience. This is significant!

Golfer's success story using the perfect balance in golf program

Bill Di Masi from San Diego is an example of this dramatic improvement, going from a six to a one handicap in just three months and becoming the talk of his club. With improved balance, Bill improved his short (chipping and putting) and long (driver) games greatly, and he had just three sessions. He is fifteen to twenty yards longer as a result of this instruction, has made personal bests of one under and two under par, and made a hole in one during the process. Wow!

> *Author's Note: The lowering of the national average for golfers can now be realized. Imagine a national average of 95 or less for both men and women. I think that target is very real. Let's go for it!*

Now for the first time everyone can play golf far better than they thought. It is our commitment to you to assist in that process with the *Perfect Balance in the Golf Swing* method. Our Mission and Motto: *Improve your balance, you improve your game!*

It's not too late to improve your balance and improve your skill regardless of age. So let's get started!

You have done the Golf Balance Test by now. What was your balance score? You know where you're at. So let's move through the steps in the *Perfect Balance in the Golf Swing* program.

> *Axiom 2: Balance is the cornerstone of the golf swing motion. From start to completion, control of the swing depends upon balance. This holds true for all rotational sports that use a club, bat, stick or racquet.*

You may be wondering at this point, "How do I learn rotational balance in my golf swing and achieve a better scoring game and more enjoyment from playing golf?" In this section lie the answers, in the form of theory and specifically designed drills to assist you in achieving "Perfect Balance" in your golf swing.

Balance awareness drills to improve golf motion

The following is a basic balance awareness drill. It will make you aware of the sensation of movement in balance, first in the feet and then in the swinging action of the arms with foot work.

Purpose: To become more aware of how your balance works starting with walking as a motion and that of golf as a lateral sport or side to side motion of the body.

Step One: Finding your balance as you walk.

Emphasis: While walking, your arms swing naturally back and forth with the motion of the foot.

As you move forward, your heel should contact the ground first and the weight of your stride carries to the middle or the forefoot, giving support to your movement. The toes give light support.

The idea here in this simple drill is to become more aware of your walking and the light swing of the arms back and forth working together with the feet and compare your personal stride in relation to this optimum movement.

Step Two: Make a side-to-side movement, such as the start of the rotational motion in golf, with your hands and arms.

As you swing your hands and arms back and forth, your weight naturally shifts from the forward foot to the back or opposite foot alternately. Notice how your foot responds and assists in the shifting or transfer of weight from side to side. You will feel a natural shift of weight in your feet and legs as your hands and arms swing lightly back and forth.

The motion of the golf swing is a swinging action of the hands and arms coordinated with the pivoting action of the body, footwork and the back right foot, which acts as the axis point to swing around.

A good example of this is a toss of the ball to a child back and forth with the arms and the body responding to its motion. This is a good example of the correct feeling in the golf swing. That's the feeling in balance we are looking for with the swing motion. Foot work plays a key role.

End Result: A better understanding of movement of the foot and lateral motion of the body in the golf swing.

Balance serves to provide an immediate sensory feedback system of the correct amount of weight that is distributed between the feet of the left and right side of the body as the golfer swings the golf club back and through. This balance motion system regulates the right amount of rotation needed in movement. Golfers will find that the more they develop a sense of proper balance in their golf game as a physical cue, the better they will hit golf

Figure 1: *Tossing a ball to a child. Notice the natural swinging action of the arms and the ease of footwork in the ball toss.*

shots creating rhythm, timing in their swings and being in communication with their target.

Balance Awareness Drill : The "Earl Woods" Balance Rocking Drill

Do this simple exercise to become more aware of your balance during your golf swing. This drill expands upon one used by the late Earl Woods to teach the correct feel of balance in the set-up and swing.

Purpose: To teach the student golfer how to feel a proper sense of balance in the athletic set up that's needed to swing the club in motion.

Emphasis: Set up to the ball in the normal way that you do and check to see where your balance tends to "list" or go to: is it towards your toes or forward, on your heels or more centered in the middle of your foot on both feet.

Stand up to the ball and get into your set-up position. Let your hands hang down forming a triangle. Rock your weight forward towards your toes and rock back towards your heels. It's natural for your balance to settle towards the middle part of the feet. Your weight should be centered more towards the middle and ball of the foot region of both feet. You should feel athletic and ready for action in the golf swing. You can do this with and without the club.

You may find this most effective if you do it with an instructor, a golf friend or buddy observing and giving you feedback on which way you may tend to lean towards in your set up.

Stress: Now move your weight towards your toes and feel how the weight is shifted too far forward. Now move your weight back towards your heels. Then shift your weight towards the middle and you will find the more ideal balance position to be set-up in your swing.

By rocking lightly back and forth from the ball of the foot to or heel, the golfer can feel that balance has to do with an even weight distribution and alignment of the knees over the ankles and middle part of the foot.

Have a golf friend or your instructor push on the right shoulder in the set-up position to set the weight inside the left or opposite foot. Now do likewise with the left shoulder to set the weight properly between the right or opposite foot. The weight should feel anchored on the inside of both feet between the ball of the foot and arch part of both feet, forefoot (ball of the foot) and heel of each foot.

In addition to this, test the weight from back to front and front to back by pushing from the opposite direction as in the above.

You will find the ideal position is to set-up with your weight centered on the middle and ball region of the foot on both the left and right foot. A bit more weight on the forefoot is the correct feeling and position with the foot for the golf swing. (More on this later).

End Result: A golfer who can feel the correct position of the feet in the set up position and in swinging the club in a balanced golf swing.

(Please Note: You have just taken the first step of the *Perfect Balance in Golf* program.)

Chapter XI

More on the Balance Principle in Golf

The importance of the stance and basic drill

SINCE THE EARLIEST formation of athletic motion and movement study, stance has been at the forefront of the training stress involved in any sports motion. Be it boxing, karate fencing, wrestling, the hammer throw, you name it, you will see the stance as the basic position to place the body in. It all has to do with being centered, and controlling motion from your center of balance.

The key stance position from these sports is the "horse stance" — which is derived from martial arts — as the foundation stance relating to alignment and balance. That is why I have selected the horse stance as the essential athletic position to build your alignment and stance in the golf swing.

This stance builds the correct position of the hip joints, pelvis, legs and feet in a strong, resilient athletic set up position with the weight centered over the lower body platform, creating dynamic tension within the legs, feet and lower back area in preparation for the motion of the golf swing action.

This stance aligns the body to the proper position for the golf swing. It promotes the key balance point necessary for the kinetic chain that results in hitting the ball correctly at high speed.

The Horse Stance Drill

Here is an important drill to develop your sense of feel and your awareness of the golf swing. This drill has three parts to it. They build one upon the other in creating the foundation for perfect dynamic balance in the swing.

This drill is for all golfers: those new to the game and those who want to refresh their balance fundamentals.

Static balance, dynamic balance and perfect balance are the goals, and this is an essential part of your training. Use it on a regular basis to hone your set-up and sense of swing motion.

Part 1: Set-up position for full swing movement

Purpose of drill: To develop a keener awareness of the athletic set-up position, especially in the lower body platform (which creates balance) and the balance centers of the body, as it relates to the essential movement of the golf swing.

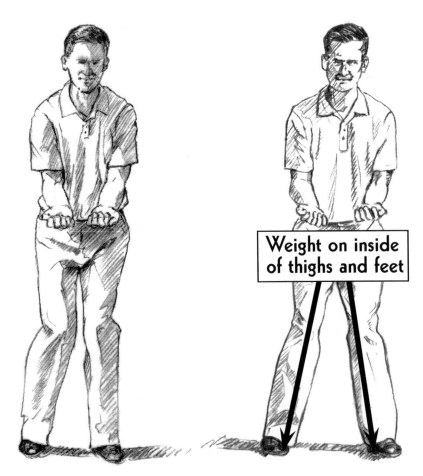

Weight on inside of thighs and feet

Fig. 1: Basic Horse Stance, taken from martial arts.

Fig. 2: Golfer's Horse Stance. Note weight centered on insides of thighs and feet.

Emphasis: Stand with the feet along side of one another, shoulder width apart. Keep your weight on inside of the feet along the balls of the foot and arches and in a readied, athletic, relaxed position.

Now drop your arms down to your sides, paying attention to the feeling created in the butt, hips and inner thigh area with the weight on the inside of the feet. Shoulders are back standing tall but relaxed.

Training Stress: Place your weight on the inside of your left and right foot with the weight also on the inner thigh knee area and with the ankle in a neutral position. This is your 'fighting' position and athletic golf stance.

Part 2: Balance Point in Golf Drill

Purpose of drill: To develop the sense of movement in support of the notion that all key movement in the golf swing comes from the ground up. To increase an awareness of one's lower body platform, especially the balance points in the feet in the golf swing.

All key movement in the golf swing comes from the ground up.

Emphasis: From a standing position without a golf club, direct your attention to your feet and locate the ball of the foot and arch portion of the foot.

Walk several feet to your right, then to your left, allowing your hands to lightly, naturally swing. Then walk several feet forward and several feet backward.

Fig. 3: "Shake hands" drill promotes a natural weight shift, with the left arm extended (backswing move).

As you do this, become more aware of the motion created by walking and your footwork and how the hips swing in synchronized motion with the feet.

Training Stress: Now make a light swinging motion with your left hand going back in the backswing to waist-high as if you were shaking hands with your golfing friend or your instructor.

From a standing position, with hands hanging down, swing your left arm across your chest to its fullest point of extension and shake the right hand of someone standing a couple of feet to your right.

Notice how with your left arm extended your weight has shifted naturally to the back foot and leg, and that the weight is centered more from the arches or ball of the foot region.

Part 3: The Hands in Your Pockets — Rocking Motion Swing Drill:

Purpose of drill: To orient the student to the feeling of moving or rotating on the balls of the feet and arches in a simple rocking motion, moving from the feet and hips.

Emphasis: The student should find that the feet and hips, especially the feet as the "drivers of the swing motion," work together as a unit and that motion from the ball of the foot and arch area is the ideal position from which to create rotation in the golf swing.

Training Stress: In this drill, the golfer places both his hands in his front pockets and creates a rhythm and tempo with his hips and feet, lightly swinging the hips within the arches of the feet and sensing the rotation back and though, paying attention to how the golf swing originates from the ball of the feet and arches and moves upward to the knees and hips region. This is a key movement of the lower body needed in the golf swing.

End Result: A golfer who can achieve and recognize a feeling of balance, who knows he is balanced in his set-up position, and can "feel" the evenness of the motion back and through in the golf swing.

These first drills were designed to increase *balance awareness* in the movement of the body, especially in the lower body and feet, and a recognition that footwork is a key component in the golf swing motion. (Footwork has been a neglected fundamental in the golf swing, yet all advanced and top golfers have excellent footwork in their swings).

> *Master Golf Swing Tip: The essence of the golf swing is balance, coordinating the movement of the body and the swinging club head via the interaction of hands, leg and feet. It is good interactive footwork and use of the lower body that is the mark of the accomplished player. You will notice that all top players have excellent coordination in the forward swing to the ball and target, utilizing balance and footwork in a harmonious fashion. This is the key to the golf swing.*

Balance Awareness Swing Drill: Practice swinging the club head back and forth with a smooth pace about three quarters, going back and through swinging the club in reps of 5-10 passes. Now do the same and close your eyes and feel the sensation of the weighted club head swinging back and thru and creating motion.

The best golfers, the pros you see playing at such a great level of play all have one thing in common: They have *impeccable balance* in the swing. This is the *primary key* to effortless power, and creates the basis for all other components of the swing to work. It is how they achieve long, accurate drives and power. They are moving the body and club in the same direction and at the same rate, which translates to club head speed and power.

Chapter XII

Dynamic Balance and Sports Motion

ONE DAY WHILE I was watching several of the top pros practice here for the Nissan Los Angeles Open, I became very interested in what "key" move they made to drop the club down, and to harness power effortlessly in their swings. I also paid particular attention to their footwork and observed how their feet played a key role in a rhythmical way with their balance.

I wondered if there was a common thread, or some truth in the myth of a "magic move" in the down swing that these world class golfers possessed. The more I watched, the more I became convinced that there must be a "move" that made it all hang together.

I remembered a passage out of my first book, *The Ultimate Game of Golf*, and the drill that I developed years ago relating to centrifugal force. The "light bulb went on" and the mystery began to unravel. The pros were keying on *mastering gravity and centrifugal force and have learned to key on that skill exclusively.* That had to be it.

It led directly to a "magic move." Make the move and you had the key to the golf swing in your possession, to tap and use time after time. Wow! *Rotational Balance* in their golf swings! It was one of those simple but powerful times when you are "looking right at it" and you know it's right.

The advanced golfer has learned to master the timing of this move with effective footwork and balance in the drop-down move! In doing so he is a "gravity master" of the golf swing. Another wow!

Although the sky was gray and rain threatened, the sun shone bright for me that day and I was eager to test this theory personally and with students. So this was what the pros did! I went to bed excited and eagerly awaited the sun opening up a new day the next morning.

And so it was. I hit balls for about a half hour that morning. It was definitely working. I felt a serenity and peace of mind about my golf swing and this new-found effective knowledge. It really worked.

I could feel the workings of balance in the swing, and it was something I didn't have to really think about. It worked on its own! I gathered a few students to work with that day to further test out the results.

In researching this theory further and looking at how it applied to golf and all other sports that require a hitting or swinging motion, I discovered the following principle to be true:

> *Axiom 15: The dynamic principle of sports involving hitting a ball with a club, bat, stick or racquet is: balanced or stabilized motion. In golf, maintaining balanced or stabilized motion around a fixed center point (pivot) is the key to shot-making and consistency.*

In other words, in *any* sports that involve hitting a ball, the primary skill involved is controlled rotation: motion that is dynamically balanced and stabilized.

This is the ability that the pros master in swinging the golf club, with Bobby Jones, Jack Nicklaus, San Snead, Arnold Palmer, Tom Watson and Tiger Woods being excellent examples.

Chapter XIII

The Timing Formula in the Golf Swing

IN MY FIRST book there is a brief discussion of this importance of sports motion and balance, along with an illustration that shows sports that are rotational in movement: baseball, tennis and golf. (*Ultimate Game of Golf*, p. 14).

There is a natural law in golf and all sports that involves the throwing or hitting of a ball to a target. This law involves the dynamics of movement of the body and the motion of a swinging club.

Each of these sports involves moving or swinging the club (bat, racquet) in a given manner, maintaining optimum balance and creating a powerful hitting motion that releases the built-up force at the ball at impact and sends it out towards the target.

The movement is essentially the same and follows the principle of moving a club, bat or stick back and through in a balanced manner from the *center of the body*, using a hinging mechanism of the arms and wrists, to create a powerful release of motion and club head speed into the ball. Centrifugal force plays an integral role in the golf swing in the release of the club as it is returned to the ball at impact.

We therefore have a law about this:

> *Any athletic motion involving the swinging of a club consists of planting, pivoting, and driving the body in a balanced position into the ball. Motion directed from the center of the body creates optimum leverage, control and club head speed.*

All effective timing comes from this interaction in an exact pattern, with balance the most important component. Recent studies on tempo and improving consistency have found that there is a precise timing pattern, especially the ratio of backswing to forward swing in the golf swing motion.

Poor balance affects this interaction of tempo with balance, and directly impacts consistency in the golf shot.

With a baseball pitch being delivered at 95–100 mph, a hockey puck being flicked at a similar high speed, and a golf ball being hit by a golf club with a swing of over 100 mph, an athlete has to use his sense of balance while his body creates terrific centrifugal force and arm speed, all in an instant.

How can a baseball player, hockey player or golfer coordinate all of the factors of hitting the ball in such a short amount of time, yet stay in control of the shot? There is no time to think about it: it has to be instinctive.

In working with golfers, from beginners to advanced touring pros, I found the better the student's skill in timing, the better the result in the shot. This is because the player has learned to build his swing around the three key fundamentals of balance, along with the tempo and rhythm of the swinging motion.

These components create a predictable timing pattern. **It is this pattern that is the key to CONSISTENCY in shot-making.**

Golfers who simply swing, and don't try to force the shot, produce a more consistent shot by being able to reproduce these timing factors. The key ingredient in the timing formula is the balance of motion and force in hitting the shot.

Therefore, *the most essential part* of the swing is focusing on this *rotational balanced* movement. With proper balance, we achieve control and feel and an improved stability of motion in our effort to hit the golf ball more consistently. With proper balance, we achieve stability in the rest of the swing factors, especially the pivot, and the club will follow the correct path.

I have observed many students regain their sense of timing and purpose in their swing, just by becoming more aware of these components.

That is why you might see the pros swinging with great rhythm at a golf tournament, pick up on it yourself, and begin to play better after the event and for the next few weeks. You eventually slide back into your old swing patterns, thinking too much about the pieces instead of simply swinging the club head with better rhythm and tempo.

Since the discovery of the above law and working with numerous students on its application, I have developed an additional formula that incorporates some of the basic components of rotational balance in the golf swing. Advanced golfers and pros pattern their golf swings around his interaction and timing pattern.

> *Axiom 7: The formula for rotational balance consists of balance, swing tempo (speed) and rhythm in the golf swing motion with the club head.*

To hit good consistent golf shots, you train your mind and body to focus on the path of the shot and maintain dynamic or rotational balance back and through with the target.

You become aware of the shape of the swing, letting the club swing back, up to the top, and down to the target and outward.

You learn to let go of the purely technical model of swing positions and focus on the path and shape of the golf swing as it flows naturally in a circular motion from inception to impact and completion.

The club head swings and flows along a predictable, consistent path in its motion around the body to the ball and outward towards the target. Let the swing flow on this path to the target.

> *Master Golf Swing Tip: Good Balance and swinging the club head at a comfortable pace gives you control. It works in harmony with tempo and controls the sense of timing in the golf swing. Hitting more consistent golf shots is a direct result of this stability of balance in the golf swing. Control comes initially from balance and good footwork.*

Mechanics, the technical aspects of the golf swing, are an essential part of learning the fundamentals of stance, alignment, grip and the path of the golf swing back and through. These are learned actions that become instinctive and eventually become secondary in importance to the sensory "feel" game, which always maintains attention on and communication with the target.

Once the scale to the piano is learned as a pattern it becomes second nature in thought. The same holds true with the flowing nature of the golf swing. Just as you practice the piano scale with a series of drills to keep the feel going, it is the same with the golf club in practicing the golf swing motion, back and though.

The primary swing skill is feeling this balanced motion in relation to the weight of the swinging club head and coordinating these together as one.

Remember this one! *Make it your primary swing focus.* Keep it in your golf journal and in your golf bag. Play out its rhythm. It has a special quality, timing and dimension all its own and is the "music" you have been waiting for in your golf game. A golfer "keeps time" with his feet, and the intrinsic music of the golf swing is its rhythm and the *swoosh* of the ball at impact.

> *Axiom 10:* *All well executed golf shots are the result of swinging in dynamic or rotational balance from start to completion in the golf swing motion.*
>
> *Corollary:* *All poorly executed golf shots are the result of swinging out of dynamic balance from the beginning of the swing to its completion.*

This skill can be improved step by step through drilling, by feeling two motions working together while you let go of the mechanical principles that limit your awareness of balance during the golf swing: *The hands and arms swing upwards on a Ferris-wheel shaped plane, and the shoulders and hips rotate on a horizontal plane, similar to a merry-go-round.* (See opposite.)

> *Master Golf Swing Tip:* *The golfer's main swing key is feeling a sense of balance in relation to the weight of the swinging club head and coordinating these two actions and motions together as one. The club is swung back in the back swing motion, moves up to the top of*

Figure 1: *Swinging in rotational balance is the golfer's key focus!*

the backswing, and comes down and through to the target. Think of the path of the swing as circular.

It is vital to acquire "feel" by practicing swinging the club, utilizing the weight of the club head in the swing motion. This is the most important characteristic of the swing motion of the golf club and is the make or break point for the golfer in developing a sound, efficient swing.

The legendary Sam Snead, considered by many to have the best tempo and swing in the game, swung the golf club back and through as many as 100 times a day, grooving in this particular feeling of the club head rotating with the arms swinging and leading the way. This was one of his keys to success as a golfer.

I have incorporated it into a drill here because of its workability and the success I have seen using it with students. It also has been a popular drill in several golf schools here in the U.S.

As a golf teacher, I consider this drill to be one of the top swing drills of all time. It is very effective and will pay dividends for you if you do it several times a week, if not daily.

Here is the Sam Snead Drill:

The Sam Snead "Old Smoothie" Drill for perfect balance in the golf swing

Purpose: To train the golfer to focus on just swinging the club head back and through in a balanced rhythmic manner while feeling the weight of the club head being swung.

Emphasis: Swing the golf club; just free swing it back and through coordinating balance and rhythm. Start with sets of five swings, swinging back and through in continuous motion with a smooth swing pace. Work up to higher sets of 10, 15 or 20 swings in a set. Swing the club on a daily basis, swinging in sets. A small weight can be added, but the purpose of this drill is to feel the club head weight swinging back and through, becoming more

aware of the sense of gravity, so don't add more than one or two pounds of weight in the swinging of the club to prevent possible injury.

Result: A golfer who is more aware of the feeling of the weighted club head and can maintain his sense of *balance* and *feel* in the golf swing motion.

> *Master Golf Swing Tip: Each golfer has a particular speed or tempo that works best for him that is tied to his sense of balance or swing. You can find your swing tempo by swinging the golf club in the following manner. Raise or hover the golf club off the ground about six inches and free swing the club back and through, making full swings with a driver or three wood. Now make full swings focusing on your ability to maintain your balance. You will find by swinging at about 75-80% that you can maintain your balance in a more stable manner comfortably – "swing between the arches"— control your swing, and accelerate your arms and hands more through the ball at impact.*

You can make this into a swing drill and work on this at the golf range or on the golf course. Excellent tip.

Chapter XIV

The Three Major Actions in the Golf Swing: Plant, Pivot and Drive

Axiom 8: There are three primary actions in the golf swing that are interactive. These are planting, pivoting and driving and each one affects the other two.

THIS INFORMATION WAS first noted and recorded in *The Ultimate Game of Golf* and used successfully by many of my students and those who read this work. It was based on observation of the pros I have worked with on tour.

If you fully grasp these three actions of the golf swing and can apply this information as a student, along with the information on balance and foot-work, you will be an advanced player capable of single digit scoring.

To fully understand these three aspects of the golf swing motion and how they work, let's look at each part individually, then how they interact.

Planting

Planting is the action of setting up the body in a stabilized position in preparation to swing and strike the ball. This is the ideal athletic set-up position for the body to assume, beginning at address and continuing throughout the golf swing.

As earlier discussed, the "horse stance" as used in martial arts, is the foundation from which is derived speed and controlled power. This stance supports the balanced movement away from the center and fully supports the quick, explosive accelerated move at the bottom of the swing at the ball.

I began to incorporate this into the set-up, pelvic and spine angle positions of my advanced players in the early 1990s.

The function and feel of the horse-stance from the martial arts, especially aikido and Tai-Chi, create the right athletic platform in the lower body and its quick, accelerated move or thrust towards the ball at impact.

Planting refers to the athletic position of the body not only at set-up but throughout the golf swing. The latest research that I have done in this area indicates the importance of this athletic position to achieve proper balance from start to finish in the swing.

Pivoting

Pivoting is the action of rotating the torso around the spine, back leg and foot in the golf swing. This creates tensional coil. This action, and how it actually *generates* power, was found to be one of the chief misunderstood aspects of the golf swing. This lack of understanding creates many errors and the need for compensation of various sorts in the swing.

The pivot begins at the ball and upper arch regions of the left and right foot. It generates rotation in the foot and ankle area, which then relays the rotational coiling motion in a chain reaction fashion upwards to the rest of the body.

The hips and shoulders rotate in rapid succession and provide support for the arms and hands in creating a whip-like rotational motion around the body in the downswing, which is released at impact.

Driving

Driving is the action of accelerating the lower body motion with the club towards the left quickly and forcibly towards impact with the ball. It is the effort to drive at the ball, with a velocity or speed one can control, in a well-timed fashion. This is what creates explosive, effortless power.

(We will examine Pivoting and Driving in more detail in the next two chapters).

Chapter XV

Balance and Pivot
Work Hand in Hand

AN UNDERSTANDING OF balance in the golf swing begins with understanding the role of the pivot action. The pivot depends upon footwork and its relationship to maintaining optimum balance throughout the golf swing.

Although balance is the number one weakness in fundamental application found in our surveys, pivot ranks a close second as the most misunderstood action in the golf swing motion. 90% of all golfers, including numerous instructors, cannot define or demonstrate a proper pivot.

Approximately 50% of all golfers have some form of reverse pivot action—an action of the turn or coil in the golf swing in which the golfer swings off of his back leg in the follow through because of incorrect balance—that prevents them from swinging correctly.

In many cases, this is due to the fact that as students they never learned what pivot meant in the first place. And it was never really defined or demonstrated to them by the instructor, who probably also had a weak point on its application.

All right. Let's understand better the why the pivot is a key action in the golf swing, and what it is.

Defining pivot in the golf swing

A pivot is *a rotational movement around a fixed point or axis.* This is a vital point in understanding and achieving a smooth, natural and powerful golf swing, because you have to know what those fixed points are in order to achieve proper rotation around them.

The pivot in the golf swing sets up stability of motion of the body and the proper degree of rotation of the lower body, torso and arms in relation to the body's fixed points of balance.

A faulty pivoting action is a direct cause of inconsistency in the golf swing. The degree to which the student can maintain balance and pivot determines the quality and integrity of the golf shot.

Pivot points and rotation

The torso rotates on a horizontal plane during the golf swing – the pivot points in the left and right foot provide the support and balance for this rotational path to be maintained.

The arms swing along a more vertical (up and down) plane and the combination of these two movements creates a three dimensional plane. In the mechanically-oriented teaching model, the path of the swing has been subordinated in importance to *swing plane*. It is highly technical, and has created a population of golfers who are fixated on and cannot perform this swing action. This demand to "swing on plane" by instructors has contributed to frustration, failure and an exodus of students from the game of golf.

The first key is to establish a reference point or position around which to turn or rotate. This will either be the spine for the "modern day swing", or the inner right knee and ball of the foot for the "classic swing".

The pivot action

A properly executed pivot action initiates stabilized rotation and balance during the golfer's swing movement. A poorly executed pivot action will throw a golfer off balance during his swing. All the common and most important errors in the golf swing result from faulty pivot action and balance.

The pivot action begins in the ball of the foot. The left foot pivots by rotating or turning inward while the back (right) foot receives the weight and is the fixed pivot point. This pivot action allows the arms, mid- and upper-body positions to rotate around the hips to a greater degree, creating a tight coil through to the top of the backswing.

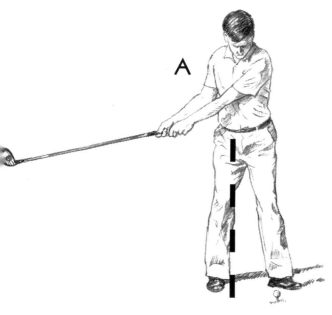

Figure 1: Pivoting around the back foot and inner right thigh.

With earlier observation and investigation, we found that eighty percent of the errors in the golf swing came about from a faulty takeaway during the first 24–36 inches of the action. With further investigation using the high speed motion system, it was discovered that the primary error in the golf swing occurred *within the first six to twelve inches in the takeaway* from the ball!

Golfers who pivot in reverse have trouble with inconsis-

tent shots. They twist or roll their weight too quickly, shifting it off the ball of the left foot towards the back part of the back foot, instead of allowing the left shoulder to shift the weight via the torso to the right leg.

This creates an unstable base for the back foot. Pivoting in this way throws the weight too rapidly to the knee, hip and leg regions. The golfer attempts to generate power using the left side of the body as the rotational axis from which to pivot, instead of using the right leg and side as the correct pivot point.

This then causes them to fall back at impact with their weight on the right side of their

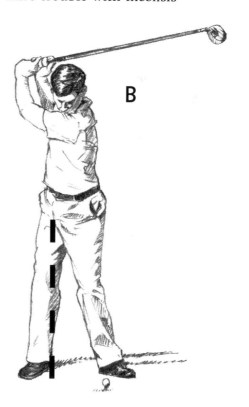

Figure 2: Reverse Pivot

In the backswing   *In the follow-through*

body instead of being able to drive in towards the left side and have a powerful surge of energy at impact.

The high speed motion analysis showed that these golfers swing the club behind the body quickly, leaving the left knee "stuck" pointing toward the ball, which is a swing error. Adding to this error, the right hip becomes over-extended and the right leg straightens instead of creating a bracing action and consequently locks the right leg, knee and thigh area as well as throwing off the spine angle. (See Figure 4.)

Important Note: Over 85–90% of golfers are making the wrong swing move in the backswing. By the top of their swings they have deviated from

Figure 3: Swing Position 1 at waist high — correct pivot

their swing's center of balance (pelvic region of lower body platform), have altered their spine angle and are off the plane or path of the swing.

This is the *real reason for inconsistency and inability to square up the club head at impact*. At downswing speeds, it is impossible to compensate club and body position quickly enough to correct the error.

See Figure 4 (next page) for the effect of correct pivot on the golfer's position at the top of the swing.

Figure 4: At top of golf swing golfer has turned, or coiled, around his inner right thigh and right foot in the backswing, pivoting around his body.

Transferring weight in the golf swing

Axiom 19: *Weight shift comes about from the action of pivoting, rotation and timing in the golf swing motion.*

The pivot action and weight shift are two aspects of the golf swing that are generally misunderstood by both students and instructors, opening the door to continuous confusion and lack of results.

Poor pivot action, especially twisting and turning of the lower body too abruptly, leads to incorrect weight shift and swaying. This results in the

Figure 5: *Reverse pivot — right leg locked with right hip over-extended*

golfer "throwing" the club at the top of the swing, "out of synch" with his timing pattern, losing potential power.

Many instructors and some seasoned golf schools teach students to shift weight laterally with the hips too early in the takeaway. With this approach, the intrinsic feel of the feet acting as the stabilizers and balance points of the lower body platform is lost. This throws the timing pattern out of sequence.

This is one of the principal reasons golfers can't improve their golf swing and scores. *Weight shift comes from pivot action, rotation and timing in the golf swing motion.* It is a *natural response* when these actions are executed properly with the weight centered between the feet. Weight shift is in actuality a direct, natural function of pivot, rotation and timing in the golf swing motion. It comes about when the swing center is shifted between the arch and ball of the foot of the feet in the backswing motion.

The left shoulder rotates back towards the golfer's chin in the backswing move and moves forwards towards the ball in the forward swing motion and in the follow through. In this way the golfer's swing center is rotated between the inner part of his feet in the golf swing.

How fast he rotates back and forth determines the speed of the swing. Advanced golfers will have ninety degrees of rotation or more at the top of the backswing with the left shoulder and arm in extension. In doing so, *the golf swing's hub or swing center, located at the breastbone area, creates a weight shift* of the upper part of the body over the lower body platform.

The legs and hips are in rotation but resisting the coiling action of the torso in the windup. This resistance is assisted by the pelvis remaining in a relatively neutral position, which helps to stabilize and hold the coil in place. The pelvic region provides stability to the pivot. It must not be over-rotated in the backswing.

When the motions of the upper and lower body are coordinated, a powerful coiling action results, with a smooth interchange of balance and motion of the club head. This allows the golfer to rotate naturally over the back leg (the axis point) of the swing and to focus on the timing of the shot.

When the upper body is pivoting in this way, and the left shoulder moves under the chin when the club swings to the top of the backswing, *weight shift occurs naturally* and efficiently. The golfer experiences perfect dynamic balance in his golf swing motion. The immediate result is more consistent shots.

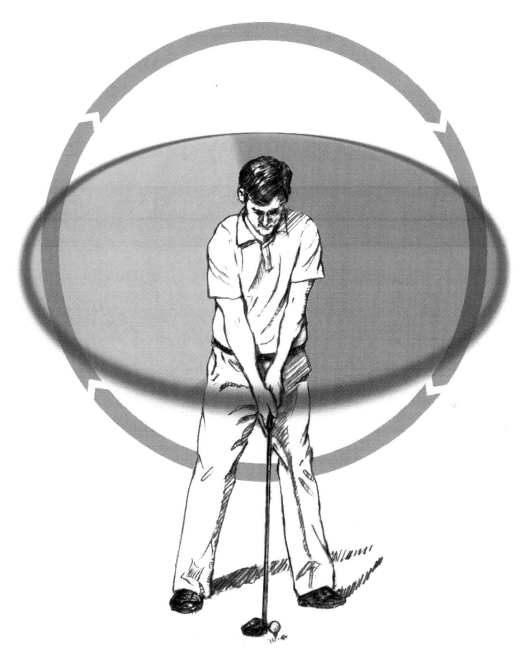

Figure 6: *Rotational balance produces a powerful coiling action.*

Chapter XVI

Drive Action in the Golf Swing

D RIVING THE SHOT to the intended target is the culmination of all other actions involved in the golf swing. All forces are in motion and interacting as the golfer swings down towards the ball for the strike.

Club head speed is produced from acceleration of the hands and wrists at impact as the arms swing the club through and out towards the target.

At the top of the backswing, the club head begins to transition and change direction. It swings down towards the ball as the lower body rotates or shifts back toward the ball at impact. The drive of the lower body towards the ball is assisted by the arm swinging motion.

This unwinding of the lower body involves the driving, accelerated action of the legs, hips and feet as they rotate through the hitting area and the arms swing out towards the target.

More advanced players find that as their hands gets to about ear level or above in the backswing, they are already initiating the downward motion with their lower body.

The swinging club head begins to square up and realigns with the forces of gravity (centrifugal force) in its downward motion toward the ball through effective wrist action as the swing center (at the breastbone) rotates back to its starting point (Swing Position 1: Address). The feet and lower body anchor the center of rotation. The club head moves out towards the target and finishes over the left shoulder with the weight firmly on the left side.

> *Master Golf Swing Tip: The change of direction in the golf swing from the backswing to the forward swing is a crucial transition. It acts from the ground up through the golfer's feet and lower body — especially the feet.*

Don't rush — pace is important

Learning to swing the golf club at a comfortable pace is the secret to a well-timed golf swing and allows the transition to occur more efficiently.

This changing of gears at the top of the golf swing needs to be smooth, not rushed. A smooth tempo is key. According to the great Sam Snead, the speed of the swing should be slow at first coming down just like the start of the back swing.

Swinging at 80% of maximum pace allows you to keep the swing in balance, controlled, and moving towards the ball and target.

The existing golf swing model places heavy emphasis on mechanical positions of the body, especially that of the swing plane, which golfers have a hard time duplicating or understanding. This is why the national men's and women's averages remain stuck over one hundred.

I think it's time we changed an instructional model that is flawed, and rediscover the true basics and fundamentals of the game. The new *Perfect Balance in the Golf Swing* method, based on natural laws and principles of motion, leads to a higher understanding and enjoyment of the game and *much* better scores.

I invite you once again to make that change.

In Part 2 you will find the answer to all your swing problems in the form of specifically designed drills to assist you in achieving *Perfect Balance* in your golf swing.

It is only by swinging the club head in balance that the golfer will learn to improve his game and control his swing motion in the golf swing. It is this skill you must master to play better golf. The good news is, from the many reports and successes we have received, that this is something you can achieve in a relatively short period of time and practice.

Part 2

Building the Perfect
Balance Golf Model

Chapter I

Learning the New Balance Principle of the Golf Swing

Balance is golf's key fundamental

FROM THE BALANCE test that you did earlier in the book, you have an idea of how your balance in golf rated from your score. Now let's take up what to do about it if your score was average, or below where it needed to be.

In my first book, *The Ultimate Game of Golf*, balance was defined as steadiness, equality of weight, amount and maintaining of equilibrium of forces. Since that time, I have made a further finding in its application to golf and the swing: the discovery of *rotational balance*.

Most every discussion of golf balance has had to do with the set-up and how to align the body to the ball and target with the distribution of one's weight, and trying to stay on balance throughout the swing to swing's end.

Expanded definition of Rotational Balance

> *Rotational Balance:* is the perception or awareness of swinging a moving weighted object such as a club or bat in relation to the body in a timed motion pattern to a target.

> Furthermore, balance is the sensory awareness of maintaining the swing's center point in motion with movement of the body and club as one in motion in the spatial plane or path of the golf swing. This is done by providing a timed, steadied pattern of motion in which a rhythm and tempo is established in the swing.

It is vital in learning golf fundamentals to acquire "feel" by practicing swinging the club, utilizing the weight of the club head in the swing motion and using balance to feel your way with the body. The advanced player uses a system of feel based on the weight of the swinging of the club head and of the body via the feet and lower body to regulate the sense of balance. We will learn more how this is done.

Master Golf Swing Tip: In other sports such as archery, the archer's attention or focus is placed on the target, not the bow or arrow in delivering the arrow to the target. The archer is rooted to the ground and learns the importance of standing to the target with balance. Likewise with the golf swing, the golfer must adapt his stance to the target and keep it steady, with the weight distributed in the feet. He can then focus his attention on the target line. This is an important point to grasp and keep in mind in practice and in actual play.

When the attention is placed on the target line, the golfer can simply swing the club on this path.

When he also maintains perfect balance, his swing's circular path will automatically send the ball exactly in the direction of the target.

Building Perfect Balance in the golf swing from the ground up

There are ten key steps to building your Perfect Balance in Golf Swing:

1. The New Set-up Position

2. Common set up errors in the golf swing

3. Key Info on Finding Your Balance Points

4. Moving from your Swing center and the Catcher's mitt Drill

5. The Pivot (covered in Section I)

6. Footwork and leg drive are vital elements in effective shot making

7. Rotational Balance

8. Effortless Power in the Golf Swing

9. The Magic Move Down

10. Driving at impact

Actually, I'll add one more. Although it comes at the very end of the swing, you'll know you are totally on balance when you achieve it!

11.   Swing's end and the Photographer's Position

So let's begin building our golf swing from the ground up. That begins with the lower body platform: the legs and the feet, which form the base.

We need a stable foundation from which to hit the ball. The lower body, especially the legs and feet, provides that foundation. To attain balance in golf, steadiness and an equality of weight are required to position the body's center of balance. With this as our base, we can use the two key forces — gravity and centrifugal force — most effectively.

The lower body platform is built upon the position of the feet, primarily on the balls of the foot where the arch on the inner side of the middle of the foot joins with the forefoot and ball of the foot.

In all your practice and play, remember that the golf swing motion is created and initiated *from the ground up.*

> *Master Golf Swing Tip: In all your practice and play, remember that the golf swing motion is created and initiated from the ground up. You will play your best golf when you lower body leads the way.*

Chapter II

The New Set-up Position

As earlier discussed in Chapter IX of the first section, the "horse stance" is the best set up position to ensure balance, centering and stability of movement in the golf swing. Tiger Woods, Ernie Els, VJ Singh, Sam Snead, Jack Nicklaus, Gary Player and Anika Sorenstam all use this.

The "horse stance" creates an athletic position from which you build your stance and alignment into the golf swing. This stance aligns the body to the proper position. It provides a solid base, a platform that allows the necessary rotation to occur in the key parts of the golf swing.

One of the best features of the "horse-stance" is that it positions the hip joints, pelvis, legs and feet so that they make a strong, resilient set up position with the weight centered over the lower body platform. It creates dynamic tension within the legs, feet and lower back area in preparation for the motion of the swing.

The key here is to create a comfortable, balanced set-up position that is stable and athletic, readied for high speed, accurate movement. The point of this position that is unique to golf is that the golfer aligns his body alongside the golf ball at address.

Static balance at set-up and alignment to the ball

THE GOLF SWING motion begins from a still, or *static*, position at address, then proceeds into a dynamic, fluid motion in which the golfer makes a swing motion back and then through to the target. Once the golfer's harnessed energy has been released, the swing comes to a rest position again at swing's end.

A key ingredient to consistency in the golf swing motion is the ability to move from static balance at address to dynamic balance throughout the swing, in a timed sequence of actions.

Static balance in the golf swing is the still or quiet balance point the golfer starts from in his initial set up to the ball. We are talking about a comfortable athletic position he assumes, aligned with the ball and target at the start of the swing. He goes into motion as the golf club is swung back.

The ideal athletic set up position is with the shoulders back and chest out, with the lower body in alignment and the weight distributed evenly over the knees, ankles, and balls of the feet. The butt is pointed slightly outward, which tilts the pelvis and lowers the center of gravity.

The weight is supported on the inside of the feet where the ball of the foot and the arch meet, directly in line with the big toe.

This creates a feeling of dynamic tension in the inner knee and thigh area as well and aligns the foot line—the ankle and ball of the foot—in a more neutral position that is ideal for rotational balance.

Most golfers set up with too much weight on the heels or towards the toes and are off balance from the start of their golf swing. This creates a need to make a quick, jerky, compensatory motion with the hips and knees in an effort to *counter balance* the swing motion which is now off-center due to an off balance set up.

Figure 1: *Set Up position (Swing Position 0)*

Common set up errors in the golf swing

Having worked with hundreds of golfers at all levels, I have observed a number of set up position errors that mess up the golf swing. They are fully listed in Chapter 4 of Part One, so we will take up only the most important ones here.

To recap, we had found that most problems come from faulty setup position, where the weight is unevenly distributed between the feet. This forces the student to create a counterbalance effect very early in the swing.

From the top of the backswing, the golfer fights this out-of-balance state all the way down. At impact, the most likely result is a poor or off-center shot.

There are three main takeaway motions that, individually or in combination, create swing errors. They are usually unrecoverable because the golf swing is so quick. These three are: over rotating the foot and ankle; left shoulder dropping towards ball; and swinging too quickly to the inside away from the ball.

Of these, two—*over-rotating the foot and ankle*, and *reverse pivot in the backswing*—are the most common. These two alone create swing problems for 70–80% of golfers.

Over-rotating the foot and ankle occurs when the student has started his golf swing predominantly with the hips. This signals the feet to make too forceful a rotation at the beginning of the backswing. The entire swing is off balance at this point *and cannot be recovered.*

A reverse pivot is a swing action or motion in which the golfer keeps his weight centered too much on his left side. He pivots off the front left foot and left leg, so does not transfer his weight properly to the back foot. Consequently the golfer "throws the club" from the top of the swing and rotates the lower body too quickly, losing control of his swing in the process.

Fifty percent or more of all golfers have some form of a reverse pivot action and swing off their back leg in the follow through, including upper body tilt.

In the majority of cases, the problem with the reverse pivot action is that the golfer is off balance in the first 12–18 inches of the move back away from the ball. This causes the golfer to over rotate his ankles, knees and hips, and to straighten the back leg, which throws off the timing and balance sequence of the backswing. This causes some major distortions, for which he then has to compensate in his swing move.

This movement away from the ball is too fast in the lower body, leaving insufficient time for the golfer to adjust his swing. He tries to whip the club and lower body around in an effort to hit the ball cleanly, but he remains out of balance and his swing out of control.

The reverse pivot action robs the golfer of power. It makes it almost impossible to time the shot correctly, which leads to the wide variety of swing errors and inconsistency we see in shot-making.

Figure 2: The Reverse Pivot robs the golfer of power in making the shot.

Master Golf Swing Tip: Some of golf's all time greats, like Sam Snead, knew that shot-making begins with footwork, and would practice <u>barefoot!</u> In doing so, they improved their sense of feel in the feet, especially the interaction between the ball of the foot and the arch area. This is a fantastic exercise that will improve footwork, timing and golf shots, and will prevent any incorrect move away from the ball in the backswing.

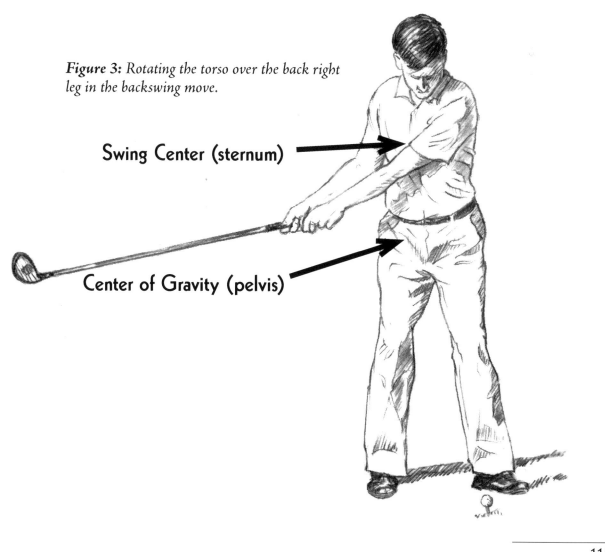

Figure 3: Rotating the torso over the back right leg in the backswing move.

Swing Center (sternum)

Center of Gravity (pelvis)

Chapter III

Finding Your Balance Points

THERE ARE THREE primary points of balance involved in the set up position and the golf swing.

The three key areas of the body that comprise the balance point centers are the top part or head region (including the ears and eyes), the middle or core area and the feet or ball of the foot area. The last is the primary control center due to its being in direct contact with the ground. It coordinates movement with each of the other balance centers.

Starting in the set-up position, look down and become more aware of your set-up to the ball. The weight should be more on the balls of the feet/arch, through the inner knees and thigh area, the first balance point.

Now find your torso and locate the center of your breastbone or sternum region, which is the next balance point. This is your swing center.

Then locate the center of your waist or pelvic area, which is the third balance point, the body's center of balance.

These three areas should all be in alignment. *These are the key balance points used in the golf swing.*

Pros and advanced players devote a lot of their practice to this: finding the on-balance set-up position to the target, aligning the balls of the feet, knees, hips and shoulders in a line that feels parallel to their target line and body line. It is only from this sideways 'horse-stance' position that the golfer can feel balanced or stabilized in his motion back and forth from the ball.

Many an advanced player begins his set up to the target and ball with his feet together to build the lower body platform with emphasis on the placement of their feet first, to create the awareness of balance needed in the swing.

The body line position is always a bit left (to the right , for left-handed players) of the target line in the set up position. It is parallel to the target line, with the shoulders and hips an equal distance to the target line.

To create perfect dynamic balance in the golf swing, the lower body platform — which includes the lower abdomen, pelvis, and the balance point of the foot — is the chief areas of importance, with the feet as the primary balance center to focus on. This is the area we are interested in here.

So let's work on finding these balance points, especially that of the lower body platform and the feet.

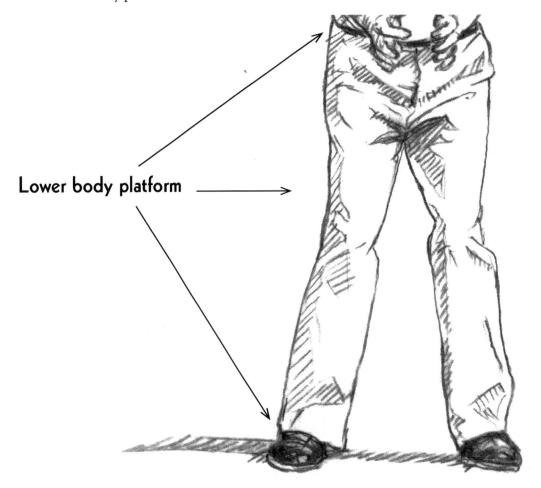

Lower body platform

Figure 1: The Lower Body Platform

How to Locate Your Balance Point Positions Drill

Purpose: To find the balance points of the body, especially that of the lower body, as they relate to balance in swinging the golf club.

Emphasis: With your feet together, form your grip and bring the club straight out in front of you just above waist high in a triangle position. Lightly bounce up and down using your feet, dropping the club down to the ground. You should feel the bounce in the arch and balls of both feet.

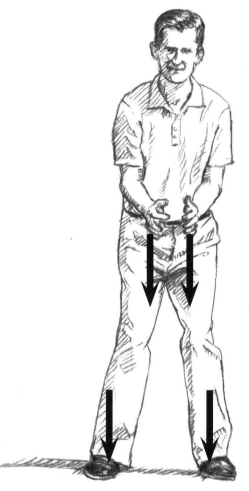

This light bouncing prepares the feet for the forthcoming rotational movement by stimulating the nerves in the muscles and tendons on the bottom of the feet. Good examples of this action are Tiger Woods, Jack Nicklaus, Nick Faldo and Greg Norman in how they position their feet at set up and how they prime these nerve ending receptors of the foot group for the athletic swing to come.

From this position, pay particular attention to centering your weight on the arch and ball of the foot area and widen your stance.

While shifting your weight lightly between the arches of your feet, swing the club back and forth a half a foot or more. From the sternum, align your upper body to the foot area with your shoulders slightly retracted. Extend your neck and buttocks naturally.

Figure 2: The key to the set up position.

Slightly bend at your hips for a better angle and rotational movement of the pelvic area.

End Result: This set-up position creates a stable base from which to generate power. It allows the player to focus on the *feeling of being in balance*, sensing the balanced connection between the upper body position and the lower body platform (core area and feet) and working both as a strategic unit.

These balance points are an important part of the pre-shot routine that the player uses in his set-up and alignment to the ball and the target. You'll notice that top players work into this particular set up position: aligning these balance points, their weight centered over their inner thighs and balls of the feet, and their buttocks positioned slightly outwards to lower the center of gravity and to act as a counterbalance to the upper torso and head.

> *Master Golf Swing Tip:* *The set-up position is an important and powerful component that allows the golfer to focus on the feeling of being in balance with the club head in motion and the timing of that motion in hitting the ball. Advanced players, especially top pros, work hard at their set ups and balance to master this position.*

Figure 2: *The athletic set-up position*

Chapter IV

Moving From Your Swing Center and the Catcher's-Mitt Drill

CHECK ANY ADVANCED golfer's or pro's swing and you will see in most cases a one piece takeaway of the arms, especially the left arm pushing away from the ball, with the left shoulder and arm working as a unit.

This sweep back of the club away from the ball creates extension in the left arm. It allows for the hands and wrists to hinge or cock at, or just above, waist-high in the backswing move. The all-important swing position must be mastered, so *practice, practice, practice* this move, every chance you get.

An additional benefit, and perhaps more important, is that it allows the golfer to maintain balance in the golf swing at waist-high, up to the top and then down to waist high as the club head is picking up speed towards the ball.

Advanced golfers work on this swing move a lot, so as to get the club in the correct position going back in the takeaway from the ball.

At waist-high, the better player will have the toe of the club head pointing up, the butt of the club or grip looking at the target and the left arm fully extended. This has the club on plane in the golf swing. VJ Singh, for example, works on this move on a continual basis.

In instructional circles, this position is popularly and known as the "catcher's-mitt" position, and makes an excellent drill (see next page).

Keeping the weight on the inside of the feet, the ball and mid-foot area, creates the vital base for the lower body—especially the hips and the pelvic muscle group—to resist the coiling action of the upper body. This interaction of the upper and lower body is what creates club head speed.

Here are two golf swings going back in the takeaway to waist-high. Remembering that 80% of all swing errors occur in the first three feet of the golf swing, we can see quite a difference.

Figure 1: Setting up the swing

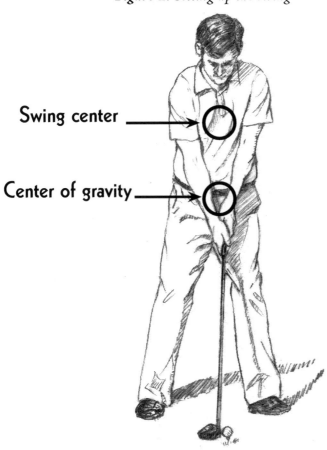

Swing center

Center of gravity

In Figure 1, we see a golfer setting up the swing, perfectly in balance. The sternum is highlighted to show the center of gravity as a vertical line down from the breastbone.

In Figure 2, we see the golfer (A) at Swing Position 2 (waist-high) with the larger muscles of the body winding up and the sternum rotated to the right a couple of inches. Figure 2 B shows the top of the swing, with full tension in the coil, weight still centered behind the ball.

Figure 3 shows the golfer in the drop-down position (Swing Position 4) with the weight still *centered behind the ball* — over the right knee, thigh and foot, but still within the arches of the feet and not beyond this point.

Note: many golfers will find that their hip turn is over-extended or rotates too much in the backswing and is outside of this line. It is okay for the shoulders to fully coil around the center but the hips must stay tighter in coil and closer to this center.

At impact (Figure 4: Swing Position 5), we see the sternum or breast-bone rotated back to center where it started from with the set-up position (Swing Position 1), returning to the center of gravity and then outward in hitting through the shot (Figure 5: Swing Position 6) with the sternum

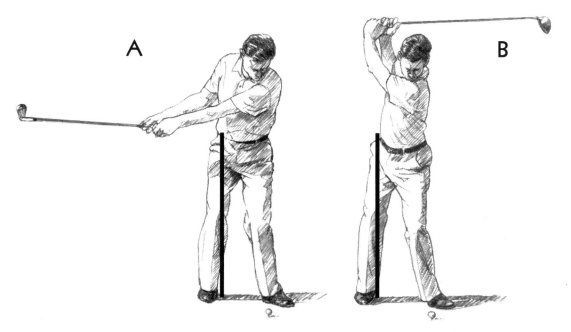

Figure 2: Swing Positions 2 and 3 – Fully coiled

Figure 3: Swing Position 4

Swing Center

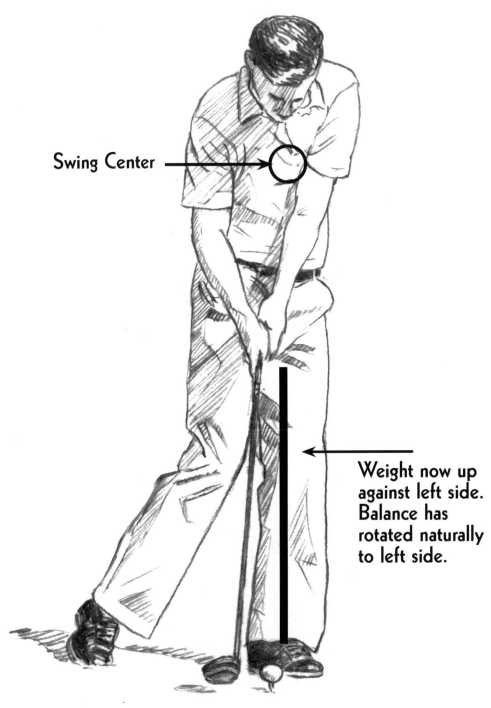

Weight now up against left side. Balance has rotated naturally to left side.

Figure 4: Swing Position 5 – Impact Position

Figure 5: *Swing Position 6 – Past Impact Move*

Figure 6: Follow Through

moving two to three inches to the left after impact position and into the follow-through position at swing's end (Figure 6, page 128).

The one-piece takeaway and Catcher's Mitt Drill the pros use

Note: Intermediate and advanced golfers should work with the club in the backswing striving to extend the left arm into a catchers-mitt image, or can use a range bucket to simulate this position at waist-high position.

Beginners should start on a gradient approach to improving this skill, using a small ball, such as a workout or tennis ball, learning to extend the left arm back. Once you feel comfortable with the drill using a ball, only then should you practice it with a golf club.

Figure 7: Swinging the arms in the Catcher's Mitt drill.

Golfers at all levels can use this drill as a good review to remedy any problems with making this part of the backswing move.

Purpose: To create the feeling of rotating the golfer's center or balance over the back foot and right leg to a waist-high position in the back swing, referred to as "the catcher's mitt position" (Swing Position 2).

Emphasis: Assume golf stance with left arm hanging down. Swing the left arm with the ball back across the chest reaching extension at waist-high in the backswing. Create the image of a catcher in baseball extending his mitt. Extend left arm across the chest into the "catcher's mitt". Left thumb is facing upwards towards sky at Swing Position 2.

Now switch and use the right arm and swing the ball back to the "catcher's-mitt" like in the above drill. Right thumb facing away from target.

Training stress: Rotate the ball over the right knee/inner thigh area to create the feeling of turning into the back leg "post" position and loading the mass of the upper body around the resisting lower body . Note: A ball of 1 lb. or so works best for this part of the drill.

As an option, the golfer can also try swinging the ball in the right hand position, swinging the ball up to the top of the back swing getting into position in the "post" or back leg position, to get the proper feel at the top of the backswing and over the back right leg.

End Result: A better awareness of the turn and the sensation of coiling the upper body over the back foot or right leg "post".

Please Note: To get the most from these balance motion drills, follow up each drill with the Sam Snead *Swing the Club Head* Drill for 30-60 seconds.

Chapter V

Footwork and Leg Drive Are Vital Elements in Effective Shot Making

Axiom 9: Footwork and leg drive are key essential balance points in the lower body platform which provide acceleration at the ball in the repeating golf swing motion.

Axiom 17: The advanced golfer interprets feel and motion via the club head, grip and feet. The feet work together as an interactive unit: providing drive and balanced support in the lower body platform during the swing, generating rotation, motion and power.

FOOTWORK IS A vital element in effective shot making and is a key component in the games of top players. You will not find an advanced player without good footwork working in the golf swing. Footwork is the key factor that affects rotation in the golf swing.

Footwork as a fundamental aspect of the golf swing has been overlooked in contemporary instructional methods. Here we take an in-depth look at this key factor in an effective golf swing.

Our focus is the ball of the foot, the padded portion of the sole between the toes and the arch.

Of *primary interest* here is the area under the first (great toe) and second toe and the padded area of muscle and tendon in this area. This is a key area of the foot that comes into play in sports such as golf, tennis and racquetball which involve a tremendous rotational, thrusting action where forward moving speed is accelerated towards a ball being propelled to a target.

The inner arch area that joins with the ball of the foot provides additional support to the ball of the foot area. This part of the foot assists in stabilizing the foot's rotational movement while hitting the ball at high speeds in quick thrust-like motions.

The heel region needs to be in a stable, relatively *neutral* position to create support and stability to the foot, especially in the ankle area, to prevent excessive twisting or rotation. This is particularly applicable in the forward swing motion at impact and out towards the target.

To achieve maximum efficiency in the swing, the golfer uses his feet and footwork to provide balance and support as he swings the club first back along the ground, then up to the top of the backswing with the arms and finally down and through to the ball.

The feet are important stabilizers of the balance, especially as the club drops with accelerated motion and force in the downswing towards the ball and outward towards the target. This has been an overlooked facet of the golf swing and is not taught in most instructional circles.

Learn it well!

Chapter VI

Rotational Balance: The Hidden "Secret" the Pros Use in the Golf Swing

ONCE AGAIN LET'S review our new definition of balance as it relates to rotation in the golf swing.

Balance is the sensory awareness of moving the ever-changing swing center point in coordination with the movement of the body and club as one unit of motion. This perception creates the swing path of the golf swing. This is done by providing a timed, steadied pattern of motion in which a rhythm and tempo are established in the swing.

Balance, rhythm and tempo add up to sensory timing, and provide the necessary ingredients to consistently-hit golf shots.

The upper body rotates around the balance point of the torso in the backswing, with the left arm and shoulder moving across or toward the right knee, thigh area and right hip. The triangle formed by the left and right arms moves further away and to the top of the golf swing.

The breastbone (swing center) rotates from the set up position on a horizontal plane. The left shoulder rotates to the right. At the top of the backswing, the golfer's breastbone should have moved several inches to the right from the start up position, and be inside or directly over the inner thigh and hip region of the right leg.

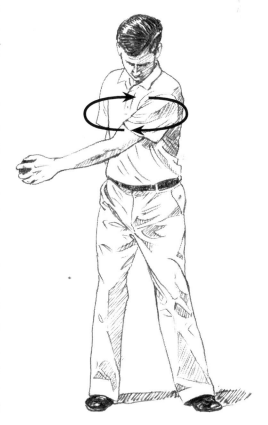

Figure 1: *Rotating from swing center in the backswing.*

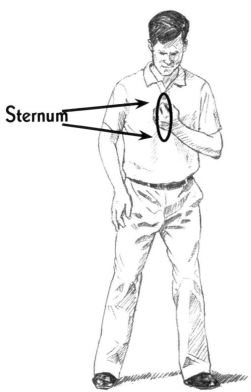

Sternum

Placing a medium-to-large size ball at the breastbone or sternum position is a good graphic way of checking to see how much rotation is occurring with the torso as you swing back away from the ball.

You can do this by taking a practice swing without the club. Holding the tennis ball with either hand, swing the opposite arm and the left shoulder

Figure 2: Set-up position with the ball at the sternum.

towards the chin. Check how much the sternum has moved to the right. This is the correct "loaded" position at the top of the backswing.

This can also be done on the forward swing, to determine the rotation of the swing center to the left as you swing through to the ball.

Please Note: We are looking for the breastbone or swing center to rotate 2-3 inches to the right in the back-swing move and about the same in the forward swing motion to impact.

Figure 3: Check how much the sternum has moved at the top of the swing.

You will notice that the left shoulder and swing center (the sternum) have rotated about the same amount going back and coming through.

As a working rule, you want approximately 90 degrees rotation with the shoulders in the backswing to the top, 55–70 degrees rotation via the hips and half of that with the knees and feet to the top of the backswing. When the left shoulder and swing center (the sternum) have rotated into the back leg and inner thigh area of the right leg. The golfer has achieved a tremendous coiling action against the lower body rotation. It is this powerful wind-up action that produces efficiency of motion and *effortless power* in the swing.

In the classic golf swing of Bobby Jones, Jack Nicklaus or Tom Watson, the rotation in the backswing is lateral or side-to-side in the lower body and utilizes more of the hip and pelvis area muscles in rotation. In the modern day position-oriented golf swing, the body's rotation is closer to the center of balance, keeping the pelvis in a more neutral position and rotating just to the right of the spine (predominantly utilizing the muscles of the torso and core region) as the axis point of the swing. The right foot and ankle remain more in a neutral position also.

The golfer is in the correct position if he has been able to successfully rotate the left shoulder under his chin during the backswing through to the top of the backswing.

Figure 4: *The powerful coil produced by the classic, balanced golf swing.*

This position can be checked by the golfer with his instructor and/or a golf buddy.

The Dynamic Balance System and Rotational Balance

Speaking of the great swings of top golfers and the role played by rotation and balance, new technology in this area is impacting swing motion instruction and giving us a closer look into the true role of Rotational Balance.

In the summer of 2005, I was introduced to the Dynamic Balance System by Dan Goldstein, an athletic trainer and this system's inventor, who was in Los Angeles at the time. He had been working with the PGA of America at their teaching and learning facility in Florida using the Dynamic Balance System.

After hitting balls and working directly with Dan and the DBS unit, I was impressed to see how my balance not only looked but felt from the feedback recorded with my golf swing. I was also able to see and study on the video monitor, how well I was able to maintain rotational balance, both static (set-up) and dynamic balance, while hitting golf shots.

The Dynamic Balance System (DBS) measures the degree of rotation from the center of balance the golfer generates during his swing and whether his weight is centered or has shifted too much to the right, left, front or back or a combination of the above. It utilizes foot plate pressure and calculates the force of the golfer's dynamic motion at various key positions in the swing. The DBS provides important feedback to the golfer and instructor on the golfer's balance, weight shift and swing center rotation during his golf swing.

I had a number of my students work with the DBS Balance Zone. The Balance Zone is a portable balance training unit that a golfer can use on his own when not working with his instructor. It is a flat balance board with foam bottom to teach in the rotational balance of the feet and lower body in a proper golf swing motion. (For more information on this unit, go to www.dynamicbalancesystem.com/cisco.html)

Years ago, Wilson Golf created a special "reminder grip" for new golfers that helped form their grip. In the same way, I am currently working on a prototype balance training device that will help golfers create a feeling of better balance to train and play with. (For the latest news and information, go to www.allaboutgolf.us/perfectbalance.html)

From working with the DBS unit I was more aware of my balance as an advanced player and pro. I knew that when I made an error in the swing, it had to do with a deviation in my balance, and I knew how to correct it. That was insightful and really made sense. The light bulb shone brightly that day!

We see the pros with impeccable balance in their swings. Using the balance principle in golf and the golf drills given in this work, you can too. You may not become an advance player or pro, but you will definitely play more to your true potential.

Master Golf Swing Key: If there ever was a golf 'mantra' or mental rhythm you should look to in your mind, it would be this one: improve your balance, improve your swing; improve your balance, improve your score. This is your new mental 'swing key' to tune into in your golf swing. Tune your game to this mental rhythm, making back and through swings.

Chapter VII

Golf's Magic Move: Harnessing Effortless Power in the Golf Swing

POWER IN THE golf swing comes from the ability to accelerate the arms and hands while controlling the increasing speed of the club head and body and the driving action of the hips to the left during the downswing, all without losing balance or the momentum of the club head as it heads towards the ball

There is a limit to how fast the swing can be, and still be under control. It varies with each player. Trying to swing flat out at 90% to 100% of possible speed is too much when it comes to controlling the club head. An out-of-control club head, even if it is off by just a degree or two, can result in the shot being hit in the rough or out of bounds.

Swinging at a 75-80% of full pace is a much more useful objective for golfers. At that speed they can maintain and CONTROL their balance effectively. Legendary golfer Byron Nelson, who led the scoring average in golf at 68.25 for almost a half a century until Tiger Woods eclipsed it, believed *the secret to control and efficiency of motion* with the woods and irons was in swinging at an even slower swing pace, around 65-75%.

The proof of the workability of his philosophy was that he was in the fairway a high percentage of the time with his driver and accurate irons to the greens. As a side note, when you are swinging well and comfortably you can "open up" with the driver and let it rip on those par four and five holes that are wide open and where accuracy is not critical.

Master Golf Swing Tip: *The secret to control with the golf swing (with the woods and irons) lies in swinging at a slower swing pace, around 70-80% swing speed. Many of the pros work on this in their practice, hitting shots with the short irons, i.e. PW, 8 and 6 iron, at different swing speeds and varying the distance they hit to, improving their swing move back and through.*

There are two vital drills that promote effortless power in the golf swing, taken from our successful Effortless Power Workshops: the classic Bobby Jones drill, and the drop-down "Magic Move" drill. The Magic-move drill is an exercise I developed for my students.

These are both very effective and get a high degree of result with students. They enable the golfer to hit longer and straighter than before.

The Bobby Jones "Feet Together" Drill

Note: Bobby Jones made this drill famous. It is highly respected and much used in instructional circles.

Purpose: This drill creates the feeling of swinging the club head more with the arms, the body following the dictate of the arms' swinging motion. A shorter stance forces the golfer to swing more in line with balance with the club head, preventing a lateral shift or swaying, especially of the hips, in the back and through swing motion.

Emphasis: With feet close or almost together in a short stance, swing the club head with the feeling of the club being heavy in one's hands. The great Bobby Jones said the golf swing motion has the "feeling of a weight being swung on a rope" by the hands. We alluded to this early in the book.

Start with half to three quarter swings to get the feeling of stable balance and work timing into the swing, swinging the arms quicker in response to the weight of the swinging club head and getting the sense of how the body turns in response to the arms' rotation.

Training Stress: Having your feet closer together keeps your hips from over rotating in the backswing move. It helps promote a shorter swing, rotation of the arms in the swing, and better footwork.

End Result: An improved sense of balance and timing in the golf swing and the recognition of the key role of swinging the arms around the body in a rhythmic way.

Figure 1: The Bobby Jones "Feet Together" Drill — a great drill for footwork.

Golf's magic move

Master instructor, Ernest Jones, in his study of the golf swing *Swing the Club Head* (1937), pointed out that the swinging motion of the weighted club head was subject to the laws of gravity at the same rate, both going up and coming down.

This is an important observation. With this knowledge his students learned to time their swing motions better, and to drop the club down (with gravity) into the hitting area. The advanced golfers improved his awareness of this, so that he perceived the weight in motion as he swung the club around his body.

The move down from the top has been a focal point in golf instruction and in many books over the last fifty years or so. It is the action point in the golf swing motion where it all comes together and the golfer "drives" at the ball with accelerating force and club head speed.

In the classic swing, the golfer gets the left heel down quickly. In doing so, he signals a chain reaction of movements — particularly of the lower body platform of the legs, thighs, hips and feet — all driving towards the ball at impact position. More modern swing technique has the golfer driving the legs and hips of the lower body up against the left side and clearing the hips to the left of target.

Learning to drop the club down and releasing the club on the downswing path correctly make a world of difference for golfers and their skill level, and has a lot to do with gathering more club head speed and acceleration. For the advanced golfer this allows the "loaded steel spring" (the shaft of the club) to maximize its unload at the ball at impact position.

This next vital drill has to do with the ability to drop the club down parallel to the target line in the downswing to the ball. It requires an understanding of tempo and timing and the laws of gravity and centrifugal force.

The Magic Move Drill

Purpose: To teach the skill of starting the downswing with the move of the lower body from the feet and lower body, to drive and drop the club down in the correct path.

Emphasis: The trick in utilizing the force of gravity in your swing is to learn how to make the transitions in your motion during the swing cycle of going back, up, down and through. To do this, the golfer learns to sense or 'time' the two primary components of the swing, which are the swing's circular path and the alternating motion back and through.

Sam Snead said that the move going back in the back swing was slow in motion and was the same for the first move down from the top of the backswing. Thank you Sam.

As the club transitions from going up to coming down towards the ball, the swinging club head has a tendency, due to gravity, to pull away from the body in the forward swing. The left arm and body sense this direction of the club head and direct the motion back towards the target line (on the circular path) at the ball. This is centrifugal force in the swing.

Many higher handicap golfers, being out of position at the top of their backswings with their weight and club position, "heave" or "throw" the club from the top of the swing and don't get the forces of nature (gravity and centrifugal force) working properly for them. This results in a loss of power.

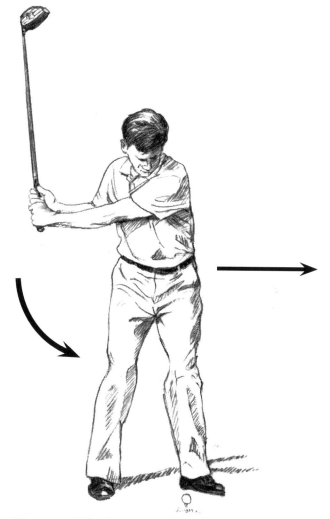

Figure 2: The Drop Down or "Magic Move".

In doing this drill, practice the timing of the drop down move as the club descends downward toward the ball. Keeping the tempo or pace consistent is important.

The more advanced player is more skilled in getting the club aligned on the correct path at the top of the backswing and allows the weight of the swinging club head to drop down with the arms and hands and lower body leading it back to the ball.

This pulls the body more towards the center of gravity, creating effortless power at the ball and out towards the target.

Result: A better drop down move (magic move) of the club head in the forward swing to the ball and target.

(I have found an excellent swing trainer that helps create the feeling of the "drop-down" move. It is the Jerry Barber Swing Developer. This is a weighted swing trainer for swinging the club head back and forth. Go to www.allaboutgolf.us/swingtrainer.htm for more info.)

Swing's end and the "photographer's position"

When the swing is executed properly the weight has returned to its original center point (Swing Position 1: Address) and shifted to the left side of the body as the arms and hands and body swing through the shot and target and over the left shoulder to swing's end.

A great image of this is the "photographer's position" in which the golfer comes to swing's completion facing the hole in 'perfect balance', in a relaxed state of comfort and stability with the weight on the left side of the body, the right toe up and foot off the ground close to the left foot, holding this position. Cameras please!

This is the ideal image you want to achieve in bringing the swing to completion. The key here is of course good rotational balance.

> *Master Golf Swing Tip: The image of the photographer's position should be tied to your mental picture of the swing's end result. Each golf shot has its own image of the finish and the ball going to the hole. It will vary depending on the type of shot, but no matter what, it will be in balance so that you could hold that position easily, say for two or three seconds, at swing's end. Lights… Cameras… Action!*

Figure 3: Swing's End: the "photographer's position". Weight has shifted naturally back to the left side in a perfectly balanced movement of club and body. Poetry in motion!

Chapter VIII

A Word about Your Most Neglected Piece of Equipment: Your Feet and Golf Shoes

YOUR FEET AND golf shoes have been the most neglected part of the physical 'equipment' needed to play good golf. Without a better understanding of the function and role of the feet and of golf shoes, golfers are at a distinct disadvantage.

The majority of golfers have not been taught the importance of good footwork in the golf swing, nor how their golf shoes, by providing the right support for maintaining good balance, play an important role in the golf swing.

Most golfers have some form of problem with their feet, either with the heel or metatarsal part of the foot, and require some form of added support from special insoles or pads to help with arch and heel support. Custom made insoles or orthotics are being prescribed more and more by foot doctors (podiatrists) to help golfers overcome such problems to meet the demands of the golf swing.

The swing is an athletic move. In the forward swing the golfer must attain a high swing speed within a very short period of time, during which there is a lot of torque or tension felt in the lower body—especially the feet. It is your feet and footwork that provide the stability and support to maintain correct balance and rotation throughout the swing.

Until recently, the quality and function of golf shoes has been lacking, and has lagged sorely behind the many other advances in golf technology such as club design and golf ball construction.

That has all changed now with the emergence of a new modern athletic style of golf shoe that is lighter, wider in the needed forefoot part, spikeless, has better cushioned insoles and is more comfortable. The newer golf shoes also have more flex, heel stabilizers, gel padding, and better arch support. It all adds up to more support, better comfort and more ability to move athletically.

The day of the traditional golf "dress shoe" design has given way to the more athletic shoe provided by such companies as Footjoy, Adidas, Etonic, Reebok and Callaway.

The function of the golf shoe is to provide stability, range of motion and comfort and the newer shoes do just that. These are important benefits for golf performance: shoes that feel good and do the job... and look good.

Golf shoe companies have done extensive biomechanics studies on the role of the foot, foot pressure, gait and motion studies, arch and metatarsal support, and heel stabilization. Additional studies on better designed spikes for griping action and traction have also been done with improved products in this area as well.

Just as the shaft is considered by many to be the "engine" of the golf club, the golf shoe is a critical component of the golfer's success by providing better balance and stability of motion.

Since the golf swing is an action that is a quick interactive function of the feet and lower body in rotation, the objective in footwork is to maintain the foot in a neutral, stable position as much as possible during the swing without losing position or being thrown off balance.

Top pros like Tiger Woods and other players are reporting that they are able to hit the ball farther, ten to fifteen yards or more longer, due to better, more athletic golf shoes. Golf shoes today are constructed to create higher club head speeds at impact, achieving more distance for the golfer.

Chapter IX

Perfect Balance in Golf — Conclusion

Axiom 10: All well executed golf shots are the result of swinging in dynamic and perfect balance from start to completion in the golf swing motion.

THIS BOOK AND its techniques are your master guide back to the golden age of golf instruction when "club-head was boss" and the golfer was in tune with swinging the club head. To a time when the golf club was truly sensitive in touch and feel and swinging the golf club was a classy feeling, joyful and momentous in celebration of the greatest game ever invented.

The legendary masters and their key students played extraordinary golf far in excess of what we would consider the equipment capabilities of the day. The first works of these great masters of the game show they knew that golf as a game had one primary objective and that was to "hit the ball!"

> *"There is only one categorical imperative in golf and that is to hit the ball. There are no minor absolutes."* The Art of Golf *by Sir Walter Simpson, 1887.*

> *"To play great golf, all one had to do was swing the club head. Generating a swing motion creates centrifugal force and perfect balance."* Swing the Club Head *by Ernest Jones, 1937.*

> *"The mission of the golfer is to develop feel from balance ... and swing the club in a balanced manner."* The Natural Golf Swing *by George Knudson, 1988.*

> *"There is only one primary importance in the golf swing and that is to swing the club in rotational balance."* Perfect Balance, *by Bob Cisco, 2006.*

The time is right to make that change and retool your golf swing using these key secrets lost to modern golf. Techniques used by the legends of the game and their teachers from the golden age of golf when "swinging the club head" and rotational balance were golf's truly magic move, golf's classic and timeless fundamentals.

With the new discoveries in balance and sports motion, and the ageless design of *Perfect Balance in the Golf Swing*, golfers of all ages can enjoy their favorite game to the fullest!

Improve your balance – improve your game! Rotational balance is your new swing key and your source of timing in the golf swing.

Swing the club head and feel the power!

Enjoy your new game.

Addendum

Breaking News — October 2007

I AM PROUD to have written and made available to you this new *Perfect Balance* book and its innovative technology: the principle and system of *Perfect Balance in the Golf Swing*. It is my hope and desire that you play better golf and reach more of the true potential you are capable of. I have always believed that all golfers could shoot in the 90s, 80s and even the 70s with the right technique, fundamentals and opportunity.

The current instructional model is not making this happen and has failed us with a national average way too high for both men and women. This has been the case for too many years now. Too many golfers have left the game out of frustration and apathy. It is time to change that failed paradigm and bring on a new, workable model. That is what we have in our possession here with this new golf program.

With the return to golf's KEY basics and the principle of *Perfect Balance*, it has been my purpose to create a renaissance in golf and if I have a mission and crusade, it is to do just that. Golf is a game that many feel is the greatest of all sports, combining physical and mental components like no other.

Due to the emergence of the Balance System of Golf and the discovery of *Rotational Balance* as a new principle of balance, I am happy to announce that a whole new field of balance awareness and sports motion has opened up to golfers. With the pilot studies we have been doing, innovative teaching strategies have emerged that are exciting and are changing the face of golf instruction.

With that in mind, and with tremendous enthusiasm and support from golfers here in the US and internationally, who have heard about and the book and its breakthroughs from other golfers, we are happy to announce that there will be an advanced volume — Volume II of the *Perfect Balance* program — with further advances, updates, drills and information. It is due out in the summer of 2008.

Please send us your successes using the new book and its drills. We would love to hear how you are doing with *Perfect Balance* and the balance principle in golf.

Wishing you much success in golf and life,

Bob Cisco

Send Us Your Successes!

W E WOULD LOVE to hear from you about your successful application of the principles in this book. Use this page and any extra sheets you need, and fax to (323) 255-3935, or email directly to the author at bobcsco@allaboutgolf.us.

We will add you to our Perfect Balance Golf School newsletter list. The newsletter is free, and contains all the breaking news to keep you up to date with advances in technique as they happen!

Name: _____

Address: _____

City: _____ State: _____ ZIP: _____

Email Address: _____

Handicap: _____ Years playing: _____

Case Histories

The Perfect Balance in Golf Program in Action

Before PBG: "I was so frustrated with my swing and thinking of quitting it was that bad. I just had a golf lesson with an instructor and it's not any better but worse. I can't do what he's telling me to do. Plus, I was starting to shank the ball.

"Then I ran into you on Christmas Eve of all times and what a Christmas present! Wow! Still can't believe the experience.

"You completely changed my sense of FEEL. Your presentation of balance as the key move really hit home to me and makes total sense and after just hitting 5-7 shots I made, I got the sensation back in my lower body especially the feet.

"I am swinging more effortless and hitting better with feel than I have in years! The ball comes off crisp and solid like it should. Wow!

"Your 'balance principle' allows me to load the swing up on the take-away and drop the club down in the follow through. Simple but powerful results.

"Thanks so much for making this a truly magical day to say the least!"

Bill Di Masi

Before PBG: Bill was an advanced player, a six handicap golfer who knew that he if could hit more consistently, he could most likely get down around par. Bill needed to improve his short game and get an extra 20-25 yards off the tee with his driver, which had become a bit of an issue due to an injury to his elbow a few years ago.

In only an eight week period, Bill went from a 6 to a 1.5 index, shot two personal bests, both rounds under par at his club and had two holes-in-one! Yes, I said two holes-in-one. This is one of the most dramatic improvements I can recall in years with students I have worked with or from other instructor successes I've heard about.

Here's what we did in his practice and training session to make such a leap.

Bob Cisco comments: Bill was not getting the full effect of dropping the club down with the driver and with "riding up" on his left side coming into hitting the ball. By getting a better set-up and an understanding of the magic move position of the lower body, especially the role of the feet and the feet driving the lower body in toward the ball at impact, his balance point was reestablished. His lower body position was now coming into the ball more on the correct path. This allowed Bill to create more of a sweeping motion at the bottom and at the ball, to move more from swing center and to rotate the lower body into the shot at impact.

Gary Beeny

Before PBG: Gary is an avid golfer who has been playing for over twenty years. He has been having recurring trouble with his swing, hits good and bad shots and lacks consistency. His game runs hot and cold and is inconsistent, though at times he hits some great shots.

I last gave Gary a lesson ten years ago, just as I was learning as an instructor more about the role of balance in the golf swing.

After PBG lesson: "Bob asked me to come in for a lesson and was enthusiastic that he could improve my game on the spot. So after hearing about his breakthrough with balance in the golf swing, I eagerly had my first contact with the "balance" concept Bob introduced as a key fundamental.

"All I can tell you is that it made total sense and I started seeing once again the simplicity of just swinging the club head in balance with your body. Shots were crisper and effortless in power and instead of thinking with all the mechanical thoughts as usual, I was hitting with more confidence!

"I had a real success with this lesson and have a real surge of hope concerning my golf swing. Now, however, for the first time I feel I have the correct information upon which to work to build a good swing.

"I am looking forward to working with Bob on the rest of the golf program to get my handicap down into single digits.

"Thanks Bob. It was all very cool!"

Gary Beeny – 18 HP.

Max Liphart

Before PBG: Max was shooting in the mid to high nineties over last five years or so.

"What a difference in feel at impact. I am actually feel the club dropping down on the ball. The shot is more effortless, going longer and much straighter.

"I found by using the information on getting my weight bettered centered on the inside ball of the foot and arch area of both feet really made a difference for me in hitting my shots.

"Thanks for the great golf lesson!"

Bob Cisco comments: Max was hitting the ball the best I have ever seen him, hitting his 8-9 irons crisply and with little effort. It was great to see, as we had become friends over the years.

Celia Milias

(Only been playing golf for a couple of years, 27 HP.)

Before PBG: Fundamentals on set up were weak and needed improvement. Swing not producing power nor consistent shots. Weight too far back on heels in set-up causing the takeaway to be too flat and to the inside. Over rotating of the hips in backswing. Scores are above the 100 range.

Celia received two lessons.

Worked first on her set-up getting her to place more emphasis on better balance in the inside of the feet and ball of the foot. Inner dynamic tension on inner thigh area as well.

Shoulders back and weight over the ankles and knees.

Celia reported a better set up routine and feeling her balance points, especially the feet, readied for the motion of the golf swing. Has better awareness of the role of the feet and lower body in the rotation aspects of the golf swing.

Starts using new swing key in game: Be On Balance throughout the shot (BOB)!

After PBG: Celia reports scores in new lower range closer to 94-96 instead of 98-105, a difference of almost ten strokes better after two sessions using the *Balance Principle* information and drills.

"Focusing on new swing key, being more aware of the role of the feet in helping with the swing motion and using a mental image of being anchored with the feet for balance helped with less frequent blow-up holes.

"Thanks, Bob Cisco!"

Max Liphart (Short Game Success)

Before PBG: Max's putting lacked confidence especially on the short putts from five feet and closer and he was three putting due to missing the short ones. He also expressed he was too negative in attitude towards his putting and needed a better routine.

Bob Cisco comments: I had Max set up in a better balanced position with his weight over his inner thighs and legs to create a more stable lower body base. This kept him from coming out of the stroke in the follow-thru to the hole.

I also suggested to him to focus on taking dead aim and stroking the putt with arms and hands to the hole as his chief objective.

After PBG lesson: It worked! Max started making these putts with more confidence and he was all smiles with the result, especially when he made two sets of four consecutive putts going in the hole.

"Thanks for the great golf lesson!"

Raymond Espinosa

Before PBG: As an advanced player Raymond could string together a number of good holes and then would have as series of bad holes where he would throw shots away to par. This was due to his set-up position being too much towards the toes which caused an imbalance in his takeaway from the ball and he would block shots to the right especially when the "heat" was on and he had to make the shot count.

Bob Cisco comments: A better set-up with the weight on the ball and arch of the foot corrected a faulty swing pattern in one session!

After PBG: Raymond's set-up position was more rock steady and in balance, which resulted in him hitting more effortless golf shots and blocking the shot to the right was a thing of the past.

His shots were crisper and more to the target as a result! Scores were improving.

Bob Cisco

Here's my own success story using the Perfect Balance System:

Before PBG: My tendency as a pro, not playing a lot due to teaching ,was to hit some inconsistent shots during the round of play that would cost me a few strokes and affect my score.

Bob Cisco comments: A quick review of the basics: better balance and keeping the weight on the inside of the feet and working on timing gets me swinging better and back in the game.

After PBG: My timing is sharper and I am hitting crisper, solid shots to the target and not losing those inconsistent shots to par. Scores are better!

Glossary of Terms

Arch (of the foot): Noun. The part of the foot that raises up or arches along the inside portion of the mid-foot between the ball of the foot and heel.

Alignment: Noun. Arrangement or position in a straight line or in parallel lines. In golf, this is lining up or positioning the club and the body to the ball, target and ball.

Balance: Noun. Steadiness, equal weight. Balance in the golf swing is both a perception and a physical orientation that controls the swing pattern from start to finish in the swinging motion of the club head. It comes from controlled movement of the body in a smoothly timed sequence.

Ball of the foot: Noun. The part of the foot that is located behind the toes that cushions the movement of the foot, especially in its rotation. In golf it is the part of the foot that controls the rotational motion of the foot, providing side-to-side strength and stability.

Biomechanics: Noun. Having to do with the mechanics of the body and movement.

Center of balance: Noun. The point at or from which all forces act equally. The golf club is swung from awareness of the motion of the body's center and the key balance points of the feet, the core region, and the head (ears). The axis point created by rotating the lower body between the arch and balls of the feet in the classic and modern golf swing forms.

Center of gravity: Noun. The balance point of the body from which the golf swing is maintained, and controlled.

Center of gravity assessment: Noun. An assessment that measures the amount of rotation the sternum or breastbone makes in the golf swing motion from the beginning of the swing to swing's end.

Centrifugal force: Noun. The apparent force that pulls a rotating mass away from the center of rotation. In golf, the tendency of the swinging club head to pull out and away from the body in the forward swing, as the rotation of the left arm and body directs the motion into a straight line at the ball. [From the Latin *centrum*, center, + *fugere*, to flee]

Centripetal force: Noun. The force from the center of rotation that keeps a mass moving in a curved or circular motion, rather than a straight line. When you swing a weight on the end of a string, your strength in holding onto the string supplies the centripetal force that keeps the weight traveling in a circle. [From the Latin *centrum*, center + Greek *petalon*, leaf]

Dynamic balance: Noun. Refers to balance in motion in the golf swing as opposed to static balance which is readied balance at set up position.

Execute: Verb. To carry out, do, put into effect in a decisive manner or way with a high sense of intention; [derived from the Latin, *ex(s), ecutus*, execute, follow to the end].

Gradient: Noun. A gradual increase of something, such as height or difficulty. In studying, gradients are used so that the student masters easier steps before progressing to more advanced or difficult ones.

Kinetic: Adj. Of, relating to, or produced by motion. [Derived from Greek, *kinetikos*, moving, from *kinein*, to move].

Kinesthesia: Noun. The sensation of bodily position. Presence, or movement through spatial dimensions. [From the Greek, *kinein*, to move + *aisthesis*, to feel].

Lateral: Adj. Side to side. In golf, the movement of the lower body back and through from a central point in the swing. [Definition taken from the Latin *lateralis*, side].

Metatarsal: Adj. The middle part of the foot between the toes and the tarsus or hind part of the foot. It is comprised of five bones. In the golf swing, this is where the weight should be centered: on the ball of the foot and arch in the mid-sole part of the foot. [From the Greek *meta*, after + *tarsos*, ankle]

Motion: Noun. The change of position of a body in space. In golf, motion is the moving of the body and club in the swing. [Derived from Latin, *motio*, from *movere*, to move].

Movement: Noun. Change of location. In golf,, movement refers to the motion of the swing and body, back and through to the target.

Positions: Noun. In the golf swing, the consecutive change of location of the movement of the swinging club head, in relation to the body and the ball.

Pivot: Verb. To turn or rotate into or around an axis point. In the golf swing, the body uses a lever system to hold body positions and rotate the swinging golf club head in relation to the ball.

Plant: Verb: To place one's body and weight in a lower center of gravity position to achieve an athletic set-up to the ball and target.

Stance: Noun. The set-up position at address in the golf swing in which the golfer stands to the ball in a comfortable position with the weight on the ball of the foot and arch, the arms hanging down from the shoulder, with the pelvis titled and the shoulders slightly back.

Static: Adj. Stationary, not moving, still (used in reference to the set-up in the golf swing).

Set up: Verb. To align the body and club along a particular line in relation to the ball and the target line in the golf swing.

Sway: Verb: to move too much to the side (laterally) in the golf swing, especially in the backswing move.

Torque(d): Verb. Twisted or loaded referring to the bend of the shaft in the golf swing motion.

Ultimate Game of Golf: The first in a series of golf instructional books written by the author, Bob Cisco. It was a best-seller.

Loved "Perfect Balance" by Bob Cisco, and would like to get an additional copy of the book?

Go to www.allaboutgolf.us/perfectbalance.html

Do you want a personalized copy signed by the author?

No problem! Bob Cisco wants every golfer to play better golf and use their true potential to improve and play their best game! Just specify who the book is for.

We would love to hear from you!

Please send us your successes with this exciting new Golf Balance Technology that is changing the way golfers play golf. We are getting great feedback from golfers from all parts of the United States and even overseas. Fax to 323-255-3935 or email bobcisco@allaboutgolf.us. Your feedback is greatly appreciated. Send in *your* success story and we'll send you a special voucher to one of Bob Cisco's next Perfect Balance and Effortless Power Golf Workshop *and* advance notice of the next book in this series: "Perfect Balance: Advanced Techniques." Call 323-255-3935 for more information.

News

Bob Cisco is preparing a follow-up book that will feature key updates to his Perfect Balance Golf Technology, the new Perfect Balance training device (due out in March 2008), and advanced drills that are getting great results and feedback from other golfers and students around the world using *Perfect Balance: Your Key to Consistency and Shot-making in Golf.*

Corporate Golfers

Do you have a group of golfers, a golf or business club that you would like to have Bob Cisco as your next guest? Then click on this link to get more info on The Perfect Balance Golf System by Bob Cisco and to have him speak at your next event or Member-Guest Invitational Golf Tournament. Go to www.allaboutgolf.us/perfectbalance.html. We specialize in corporate outings also that are tailored to your organization's needs. *Perfect Balance* can also be used as a corporate premium gift and he makes appearances at corporate events like your next sales meeting or special golf event.

College and High School Coaches

Are you a college or high school golf coach looking for key information on the role of balance and effortless power in the golf swing? Want to get trained in the new *Perfect Balance* Golf Instructional System that is changing golf instruction forever? Go to www.allaboutgolf.us/perfectbalance.html, or call the golf school at 323-255-3935 for more information. Ask for Bill Chandler or Bob Cisco. If you have a group of 8-10 coaches in your area, you can request a special workshop.

About the Author

Bob Cisco is president and owner of Perfect Balance Golf Schools, a ground breaking golf school in Southern California featuring balance and power secrets of the pros, that will transform any golfer's game to its true potential with consistently better scores.

He is the principal instructor of a series of unique workshops on the game, including the *Effortless Power Workshop*, *Perfect Balance Workshop* and *Short Game Boot Camp*, that provide expert group and one-on-one instruction for beginning, intermediate and advanced golfers.

Golfers who have read his books and who want to improve their golf games, can attend his cutting edge schools by registering at **www.allaboutgolf.us,** or by calling 323-255-3935 for more information. Special discounts are offered for book buyers and students.

Send an e-mail on your success with this book and the balance principle of golf and we will send you a special gift (audio tape or report) for responding. Our e-mail address is info@allaboutgolf.us

Designer and Editor

Alan Gilbertson of G&G Creative Productions, Tujunga, CA. (www.gngcreative.com) provides graphic design, photographic, editing and writing services for diverse clients on both east and west coasts. (818) 720 5666 or email alan@al-gilbertson.com

Illustrator

Accomplished artist and illustrator Ann Fewell is the principal of Anne Fewell Art Studio, Los Angeles, CA (www.annefewellart.com).

Email: rocketfewell@earthlink.net

Made in the USA
Lexington, KY
28 October 2017